Strength
In Time Of Trouble

The Book Of
Psalms

New International Version

STRENGTH IN TIME OF TROUBLE

THE BOOK OF
Psalms

NEW INTERNATIONAL VERSION

New York International Bible Society
144 Tices Lane
East Brunswick, N. J. 08816

PSALMS

BOOK I

Psalms 1-41

Psalm 1

¹Blessed is the man
  who does not walk in the counsel of the wicked
or stand in the way of sinners
  or sit in the seat of mockers.
²But his delight is in the law of the LORD,
  and on his law he meditates day and night.
³He is like a tree planted by streams of water,
  which yields its fruit in season
and whose leaf does not wither.
  Whatever he does prospers.

⁴Not so the wicked!
  They are like chaff
  that the wind blows away.
⁵Therefore the wicked will not stand in the
      judgment,
  nor sinners in the assembly of the righteous.

⁶For the LORD watches over the way of the
      righteous,
  but the way of the wicked will perish.

Psalm 2

[1]Why do the nations rage
and the peoples plot in vain?
[2]The kings of the earth take their stand
and the rulers gather together
against the LORD
and against his Anointed One.[a]
[3]"Let us break their chains," they say,
"and throw off their fetters."

[4]The One enthroned in heaven laughs;
the Lord scoffs at them.
[5]Then he rebukes them in his anger
and terrifies them in his wrath, saying,
[6]"I have installed my King[b]
on Zion, my holy hill."

[7]I will proclaim the decree of the LORD:

He said to me, "You are my Son[c];
today I have become your Father.[d]
[8]Ask of me,
and I will make the nations your inheritance,
the ends of the earth your possession.
[9]You will rule them with an iron scepter[e];
you will dash them to pieces like pottery."

[10]Therefore, you kings, be wise;
be warned, you rulers of the earth.
[11]Serve the LORD with fear
and rejoice with trembling.
[12]Kiss the Son, lest he be angry
and you be destroyed in your way,
for his wrath can flare up in a moment.
Blessed are all who take refuge in him.

a 2 Or *anointed one*   b 6 Or *king*
c 7 Or *son*; also in verse 12   d 7 Or *have begotten you*
e 9 Or *will break them with a rod of iron*

Psalm 3

A psalm of David. When he fled from his son Absalom.

[1]O LORD, how many are my foes!
How many rise up against me!
[2]Many are saying of me,
"God will not deliver him."   *Selah*[a]

[3]But you are a shield around me, O LORD,
my Glorious One, who lifts up my head.
[4]To the LORD I cry aloud,
and he answers me from his holy hill.   *Selah*

[5]I lie down and sleep;
I wake again, because the LORD sustains me.
[6]I will not fear the tens of thousands
drawn up against me on every side.

[7]Arise, O LORD!
Deliver me, O my God!
For you have struck all my enemies on the jaw;
you have broken the teeth of the wicked.

[8]From the LORD comes deliverance.
May your blessing be on your people.   *Selah*

Psalm 4

For the director of music. With stringed instruments. A psalm of
David.

[1]Answer me when I call to you,
O my righteous God.
Give me relief from my distress;
be merciful to me and hear my prayer.

[2]How long, O men, will you turn my glory into
shame[b]?
How long will you love delusions and seek false
gods[c]?   *Selah*
[3]Know that the LORD has set apart the godly for
himself;

[a]2 A word of uncertain meaning, occurring frequently in the
Psalms; possibly a musical term
[b]2 Or *you dishonor my Glorious One*   [c]2 Hebrew *seek lies*

the LORD will hear when I call to him.

⁴In your anger do not sin;
   when you are on your beds,
   search your hearts and be silent.   *Selah*
⁵Offer right sacrifices
   and trust in the LORD.

⁶Many are asking, "Who can show us any good?"
   Let the light of your face shine upon us, O
     LORD.
⁷You have filled my heart with greater joy
   than when their grain and new wine abound.
⁸I will lie down and sleep in peace,
   for you alone, O LORD,
   make me dwell in safety.

Psalm 5

For the director of music. For flutes. A psalm of David.

¹Give ear to my words, O LORD,
   consider my sighing.
²Listen to my cry for help,
   my King and my God,
   for to you I pray.
³Morning by morning, O LORD, you hear my voice;
   morning by morning I lay my requests before
      you
   and wait in expectation.

⁴You are not a God who takes pleasure in evil;
   with you the wicked cannot dwell.
⁵The arrogant cannot stand in your presence;
   you hate all who do wrong.
⁶You destroy those who tell lies;
   bloodthirsty and deceitful men
   the LORD abhors.

⁷But I, by your great mercy,
   will come into your house;
in reverence will I bow down
   toward your holy temple.
⁸Lead me, O LORD, in your righteousness

because of my enemies—
　　make straight your way before me.

⁹Not a word from their mouth can be trusted;
　　their heart is filled with destruction.
Their throat is an open grave;
　　with their tongue they speak deceit.
¹⁰Declare them guilty, O God!
　　Let their intrigues be their downfall.
Banish them for their many sins,
　　for they have rebelled against you.

¹¹But let all who take refuge in you be glad;
　　let them ever sing for joy.
Spread your protection over them,
　　that those who love your name may rejoice in
　　　　you.
¹²For surely, O Lord, you bless the righteous;
　　you surround them with your favor as with a
　　　　shield.

Psalm 6

*For the director of music. With stringed instruments. According to
sheminith.ᵃ A psalm of David.*

¹O Lord, do not rebuke me in your anger
　　or discipline me in your wrath.
²Be merciful to me, Lord, for I am faint;
　　O Lord, heal me, for my bones are in agony.
³My soul is in anguish.
　　How long, O Lord, how long?

⁴Turn, O Lord, and deliver me;
　　save me because of your unfailing love.
⁵No one remembers you when he is dead.
　　Who praises you from the graveᵇ?

⁶I am worn out from groaning;
　　all night long I flood my bed with weeping
　　and drench my couch with tears.
⁷My eyes grow weak with sorrow;
　　they fail because of all my foes.

ᵃ Title: Probably a musical term　　　ᵇ 5 Hebrew *Sheol*

⁸Away from me, all you who do evil,
    for the LORD has heard my weeping.
⁹The LORD has heard my cry for mercy;
    the LORD accepts my prayer.
¹⁰May all my enemies be ashamed and dismayed;
    may they turn back in sudden disgrace.

Psalm 7

A shiggaion[a] *of David, which he sang to the LORD concerning Cush, a Benjamite.*

¹O LORD my God, I take refuge in you;
    save and deliver me from all who pursue me,
²or they will tear me like a lion
    and rip me to pieces with no one to rescue me.

³O LORD my God, if I have done this
    and there is guilt on my hands—
⁴if I have done evil to him who is at peace with
        me
    or without cause have robbed my foe—
⁵then let my enemy pursue and overtake me;
    let him trample my life to the ground
    and make me sleep in the dust.   *Selah*

⁶Arise, O LORD, in your anger;
    rise up against the rage of my enemies.
    Awake, my God; decree justice.
⁷Let the assembled peoples gather around you.
    Rule over them from on high;
⁸ let the LORD judge the peoples.
Judge me, O LORD, according to my righteousness,
    according to my integrity, O Most High.
⁹O righteous God,
    who searches minds and hearts,
bring to an end the violence of the wicked
    and make the righteous secure.

¹⁰My shield[b] is God Most High,
    who saves the upright in heart.
¹¹God is a righteous judge,
    a God who expresses his wrath every day.

---

[a] Title: Probably a literary or musical term   [b] 10 Or *sovereign*

¹²If he does not relent,
  heᵃ will sharpen his sword;
  he will bend and string his bow.
¹³He has prepared his deadly weapons;
  he makes ready his flaming arrows.

¹⁴He who is pregnant with evil
  and conceives trouble gives birth to
    disillusionment.
¹⁵He who digs a hole and scoops it out
  falls into the pit he has made.
¹⁶The trouble he causes recoils on him;
  his violence comes down on his own head.

¹⁷I will give thanks to the LORD because of his
    righteousness
  and will sing praise to the name of the LORD
    Most High.

Psalm 8

For the director of music. According to *gittith.*ᵇ A psalm of David.

¹O LORD, our Lord,
  how majestic is your name in all the earth!

You have set your glory
  above the heavens.
²From the lips of children and infants
  you have ordained praiseᶜ
because of your enemies,
  to silence the foe and the avenger.

³When I consider your heavens,
  the work of your fingers,
the moon and the stars,
  which you have set in place,
⁴what is man that you are mindful of him,
  the son of man that you care for him?
⁵You made him a little lower than the heavenly
    beingsᵈ

ᵃ12 Or *If a man does not repent, / God*
ᵇTitle: Probably a musical term ᶜ2 Or *strength*
ᵈ5 Or *than God*

and crowned him with glory and honor.

6You made him ruler over the works of your
          hands;
     you put everything under his feet:
7all flocks and herds,
     and the beasts of the field,
8the birds of the air,
     and the fish of the sea,
     all that swim the paths of the seas.

9O Lord, our Lord,
     how majestic is your name in all the earth!

Psalm 9[a]

For the director of music. To the tune of, "The Death of the
Son." A psalm of David.

1I will praise you, O Lord, with all my heart;
     I will tell of all your wonders.
2I will be glad and rejoice in you;
     I will sing praise to your name, O Most High.

3My enemies turn back;
     they stumble and perish before you.
4For you have upheld my right and my cause;
     you have sat on your throne, judging
          righteously.
5You have rebuked the nations and destroyed the
          wicked;
     you have blotted out their name for ever and
          ever.
6Endless ruin has overtaken the enemy,
     you have uprooted their cities;
     even the memory of them has perished.

7The Lord reigns forever;
     he has established his throne for judgment.
8He will judge the world in righteousness;
     he will govern the peoples with justice.
9The Lord is a refuge for the oppressed,

aPsalms 9 and 10 may have been originally a single acrostic
poem, the stanzas of which begin with the successive letters of
the Hebrew alphabet. In the Septuagint they constitute one psalm.

a stronghold in times of trouble.

¹⁰Those who know your name will trust in you,
 for you, LORD, have never forsaken those who
  seek you.

¹¹Sing praises to the LORD, enthroned in Zion;
 proclaim among the nations what he has done.
¹²For he who avenges blood remembers;
 he does not ignore the cry of the afflicted.

¹³O LORD, see how my enemies persecute me!
 Have mercy and lift me up from the gates of
  death,
¹⁴that I may declare your praises
 in the gates of the Daughter of Zion
 and there rejoice in your salvation.

¹⁵The nations have fallen into the pit they have
  dug;
 their feet are caught in the net they have
  hidden.
¹⁶The LORD is known by his justice;
 the wicked are ensnared by the work of their
  hands.   *Higgaion.*[a] *Selah*
¹⁷The wicked return to the grave,[b]
 all the nations that forget God.
¹⁸But the needy will not always be forgotten,
 nor the hope of the afflicted ever perish.

¹⁹Arise, O LORD, let not man triumph;
 let the nations be judged in your presence.
²⁰Strike them with terror, O LORD;
 let the nations know they are but men. *Selah*

Psalm 10[c]

¹Why, O LORD, do you stand far off?
 Why do you hide yourself in times of trouble?

---

a 16 Or *Meditation;* possibly a musical notation
b 17 Hebrew *Sheol*
c Psalms 9 and 10 may have been originally a single acrostic
poem, the stanzas of which begin with the successive letters of
the Hebrew alphabet. In the Septuagint they constitute one psalm.

²In his arrogance the wicked man hunts down the
  weak,
   who are caught in the schemes he devises.
³He boasts of the cravings of his heart;
   he blesses the greedy and reviles the LORD.
⁴In his pride the wicked does not seek him;
   in all his thoughts there is no room for God.
⁵His ways are always prosperous;
   he is haughty and your laws are far from him;
   he sneers at all his enemies.
⁶He says to himself, "Nothing will shake me;
   I'll always be happy and never have trouble."
⁷His mouth is full of curses and lies and threats;
   trouble and evil are under his tongue.
⁸He lies in wait near the villages;
   from ambush he murders the innocent,
   watching in secret for his victims.
⁹He lies in wait like a lion in cover;
   he lies in wait to catch the helpless;
   he catches the helpless and drags them off in
     his net.
¹⁰His victims are crushed, they collapse;
   they fall under his strength.
¹¹He says to himself, "God has forgotten;
   he covers his face and never sees."

¹²Arise, LORD! Lift up your hand, O God.
   Do not forget the helpless.
¹³Why does the wicked man revile God?
   Why does he say to himself,
   "He won't call me to account"?
¹⁴But you, O God, do see trouble and grief;
   you consider it to take it in hand.
 The victim commits himself to you;
   you are the helper of the fatherless.
¹⁵Break the arm of the wicked and evil man;
   call him to account for his wickedness
   that would not be found out.

¹⁶The LORD is King for ever and ever;
   the nations will perish from his land.

[17]You hear, O Lord, the desire of the afflicted;
   you encourage them, and you listen to their cry,
[18]defending the fatherless and the oppressed,
   in order that man, who is of the earth, may
      terrify no more.

Psalm 11

For the director of music. Of David.

[1]In the Lord I take refuge.
   How then can you say to me:
   "Flee like a bird to your mountain.
[2]For look, the wicked bend their bows;
   they set their arrows against the strings
to shoot from the shadows
   at the upright in heart.
[3]When the foundations are being destroyed,
   what can the righteous do[a]?"

[4]The Lord is in his holy temple;
   the Lord is on his heavenly throne.
 He observes the sons of men;
   his eyes examine them.
[5]The Lord examines the righteous,
   but the wicked[b] and those who love violence
   his soul hates.
[6]On the wicked he will rain
   fiery coals and burning sulfur;
   a scorching wind will be their lot.

[7]For the Lord is righteous,
   he loves justice;
   upright men will see his face.

Psalm 12

For the director of music. According to *sheminith*.[c] A psalm of
David.

[1]Help, Lord, for the godly are no more;
   the faithful have vanished from among men.

[a]3 Or *what is the Righteous One doing*
[b]5 Or *The Lord, the Righteous One, examines the wicked,* /
[c]Title: Probably a musical term

²Everyone lies to his neighbor;
    their flattering lips speak with deception.

³May the LORD cut off all flattering lips
    and every boastful tongue
⁴that says, "We will triumph with our tongues;
    we own our lipsᵃ—who is our master?"

⁵"Because of the oppression of the weak
    and the groaning of the needy,
I will now arise," says the LORD.
    "I will protect them from those who malign
      them."
⁶And the words of the LORD are flawless,
    like silver refined in a furnace of clay,
    purified seven times.

⁷O LORD, you will keep us safe
    and protect us from such people forever.
⁸The wicked freely strut about
    when what is vile is honored among men.

Psalm 13

For the director of music. A psalm of David.

¹How long, O LORD? Will you forget me forever?
    How long will you hide your face from me?
²How long must I wrestle with my thoughts
    and every day have sorrow in my heart?
    How long will my enemy triumph over me?

³Look on me and answer, O LORD my God.
    Give light to my eyes, or I will sleep in death;
⁴my enemy will say, "I have overcome him,"
    and my foes will rejoice when I fall.

⁵But I trust in your unfailing love;
    my heart rejoices in your salvation.
⁶I will sing to the LORD,
    for he has been good to me.

ᵃ4 Or / our lips are our plowshares

Psalm 14

For the director of music. Of David.

¹The fool[a] says in his heart,
    "There is no God."
They are corrupt, their deeds are vile;
    there is no one who does good.

²The LORD looks down from heaven
    on the sons of men
to see if there are any who understand,
    any who seek God.
³All have turned aside,
    they have together become corrupt;
there is no one who does good,
    not even one.

⁴Will evildoers never learn—
    those who devour my people as men eat bread
    and who do not call on the LORD?
⁵There they are, overwhelmed with dread,
    for God is present in the company of the
        righteous.
⁶You evildoers frustrate the plans of the poor,
    but the LORD is their refuge.

⁷Oh, that salvation for Israel would come out of
        Zion!
    When the LORD restores the fortunes of his
        people,
    let Jacob rejoice and Israel be glad!

Psalm 15

A psalm of David.

¹LORD, who may dwell in your sanctuary?
    Who may live on your holy hill?

²He whose walk is blameless
    and who does what is righteous,
who speaks the truth from his heart

a 1 The Hebrew words rendered *fool* in Psalms denote one who is
morally deficient.

³   and has no slander on his tongue,
who does his neighbor no wrong
     and casts no slur on his fellow man,
⁴who despises a vile man
     but honors those who fear the LORD,
who keeps his oath
     even when it hurts,
⁵who lends his money without usury
     and does not accept a bribe against the
          innocent.

He who does these things
     will never be shaken.

Psalm 16

A *miktam*^a of David.

¹Keep me safe, O God,
     for in you I take refuge.

²I said to the LORD, "You are my Lord;
     apart from you I have no good thing."
³As for the saints who are in the land,
     they are the glorious ones in whom is all my
          delight.^b
⁴The sorrows of those will increase
     who run after other gods.
I will not pour out their libations of blood
     or take up their names on my lips.

⁵LORD, you have assigned me my portion and my
          cup;
     you have made my lot secure.
⁶The boundary lines have fallen for me in pleasant
          places;
     surely I have a delightful inheritance.

⁷I will praise the LORD, who counsels me;
     even at night my heart instructs me.
⁸I have set the LORD always before me.

---

^a Title: Probably a literary or musical term
^b 3 Or *As for the pagan priests who are in the land / and the nobles in whom all delight, I said:*

Because he is at my right hand,
I will not be shaken.

⁹Therefore my heart is glad and my tongue
rejoices;
my body also will rest secure,
¹⁰because you will not abandon me to the grave,ᵃ
nor will you let your Holy Oneᵇ see decay.
¹¹You have made knownᶜ to me the path of life;
you will fill me with joy in your presence,
with eternal pleasures at your right hand.

Psalm 17

A prayer of David.

¹Hear, O Lᴏʀᴅ, my righteous plea;
listen to my cry.
Give ear to my prayer—
it does not rise from deceitful lips.
²May my vindication come from you;
may your eyes see what is right.

³Though you probe my heart and examine me at
night,
though you test me, you will find nothing;
I have resolved that my mouth will not sin.
⁴As for the deeds of men—
by the word of your lips
I have kept myself
from the ways of the violent.
⁵My steps have held to your paths;
my feet have not slipped.

⁶I call on you, O God, for you will answer me;
give ear to me and hear my prayer.
⁷Show the wonder of your great love,
you who save by your right hand
those who take refuge in you from their foes.
⁸Keep me as the apple of your eye;
hide me in the shadow of your wings
⁹from the wicked who assail me,

ᵃ 10 Hebrew *Sheol*   ᵇ 10 Or *your faithful one*
ᶜ 11 Or *you will make*

from my mortal enemies who surround me.

[10]They close up their callous hearts,
and their mouths speak with arrogance.
[11]They have tracked me down, they now surround
me,
with eyes alert, to throw me to the ground.
[12]They are like a lion hungry for prey,
like a great lion crouching in cover.

[13]Rise up, O Lord, confront them, bring them
down;
rescue me from the wicked by your sword.
[14]O Lord, by your hand save me from such men,
from men of this world whose reward is in this
life.

You still the hunger of those you cherish;
their sons have plenty,
and they store up wealth for their children.
[15]And I—in righteousness I will see your face;
when I awake, I will be satisfied with seeing
your likeness.

Psalm 18

For the director of music. Of David the servant of the Lord. He
sang to the Lord the words of this song when the Lord delivered
him from the hand of all his enemies and from the hand of Saul.
He said:

[1]I love you, O Lord, my strength.

[2]The Lord is my rock, my fortress and my
deliverer;
my God is my rock, in whom I take refuge.
He is my shield and the horn[a] of my salvation,
my stronghold.
[3]I call to the Lord, who is worthy of praise,
and I am saved from my enemies.

[4]The cords of death entangled me;
the torrents of destruction overwhelmed me.
[5]The cords of the grave[b] coiled around me;

a 2 *Horn* here symbolizes strength.   b 5 Hebrew *Sheol*

the snares of death confronted me.
⁶In my distress I called to the LORD;
   I cried to my God for help.
 From his temple he heard my voice;
   my cry came before him, into his ears.

⁷The earth trembled and quaked,
   and the foundations of the mountains shook;
   they trembled because he was angry.
⁸Smoke rose from his nostrils;
   consuming fire came from his mouth,
   burning coals blazed out of it.
⁹He parted the heavens and came down;
   dark clouds were under his feet.
¹⁰He mounted the cherubim and flew;
   he soared on the wings of the wind.
¹¹He made darkness his covering, his canopy
         around him—
   the dark rain clouds of the sky.
¹²Out of the brightness of his presence clouds
         advanced,
   with hailstones and bolts of lightning.
¹³The LORD thundered from heaven;
   the voice of the Most High resounded.ᵃ
¹⁴He shot his arrows and scattered ⌊the enemies⌋,
   great bolts of lightning and routed them.
¹⁵The valleys of the sea were exposed
   and the foundations of the earth laid bare
 at your rebuke, O LORD,
   at the blast of breath from your nostrils.

¹⁶He reached down from on high and took hold of
         me;
   he drew me out of deep waters.
¹⁷He rescued me from my powerful enemy,
   from my foes, who were too strong for me.
¹⁸They confronted me in the day of my disaster,
   but the LORD was my support.

ᵃ 13 Some Hebrew manuscripts and Septuagint (see also 2 Samuel
22:14); most Hebrew manuscripts *resounded, / amid hailstones and
bolts of lightning*

¹⁹He brought me out into a spacious place;
    he rescued me because he delighted in me.

²⁰The LORD has dealt with me according to my
       righteousness;
    according to the cleanness of my hands he has
       rewarded me.
²¹For I have kept the ways of the LORD;
    I have not done evil by turning from my God.
²²All his laws are before me;
    I have not turned away from his decrees.
²³I have been blameless before him
    and have kept myself from sin.
²⁴The LORD has rewarded me according to my
       righteousness,
    according to the cleanness of my hands in his
       sight.

²⁵To the faithful you show yourself faithful,
    to the blameless you show yourself blameless,
²⁶to the pure you show yourself pure,
    but to the crooked you show yourself shrewd.
²⁷You save the humble
    but bring low those whose eyes are haughty.
²⁸You, O LORD, keep my lamp burning;
    my God turns my darkness into light.
²⁹With your help I can advance against a troop[a];
    with my God I can scale a wall.

³⁰As for God, his way is perfect;
    the word of the LORD is flawless.
 He is a shield
    for all who take refuge in him.
³¹For who is God besides the LORD?
    And who is the Rock except our God?
³²It is God who arms me with strength
    and makes my way perfect.
³³He makes my feet like the feet of a deer;
    he enables me to stand on the heights.
³⁴He trains my hands for battle;
    my arms can bend a bow of bronze.

[a] 29 Or *can run through a barricade*

35You give me your shield of victory,
    and your right hand sustains me;
    you stoop down to make me great.
36You broaden the path beneath me,
    so that my ankles do not turn.

37I pursued my enemies and overtook them;
    I did not turn back till they were destroyed.
38I crushed them so that they could not rise;
    they fell beneath my feet.
39You armed me with strength for battle;
    you made my adversaries bow at my feet.
40You made my enemies turn their backs in flight,
    and I destroyed my foes.
41They cried for help, but there was no one to save
        them—
    to the LORD, but he did not answer.
42I beat them as fine as dust borne on the wind;
    I poured them out like mud in the streets.

43You have delivered me from the attacks of the
        people;
    you have made me the head of nations;
    people I did not know are subject to me.
44As soon as they hear me, they obey me;
    foreigners cringe before me.
45They all lose heart;
    they come trembling from their strongholds.

46The LORD lives! Praise be to my Rock!
    Exalted be God my Savior!
47He is the God who avenges me,
    who subdues nations under me,
48   who saves me from my enemies.
  You exalted me above my foes;
    from violent men you rescued me.
49Therefore I will praise you among the nations, O
        LORD;
    I will sing praises to your name.
50He gives his king great victories;
    he shows unfailing kindness to his anointed,
    to David and his descendants forever.

Psalm 19

For the director of music. A psalm of David.

[1]The heavens declare the glory of God;
 the skies proclaim the work of his hands.
[2]Day after day they pour forth speech;
 night after night they display knowledge.
[3]There is no speech or language
 where their voice is not heard.[a]
[4]Their voice[b] goes out into all the earth,
 their words to the ends of the world.

In the heavens he has pitched a tent for the sun,
[5] which is like a bridegroom coming forth from
  his pavilion,
 like a champion rejoicing to run his course.
[6]It rises at one end of the heavens
 and makes its circuit to the other;
 nothing is hidden from its heat.

[7]The law of the LORD is perfect,
 reviving the soul.
The statutes of the LORD are trustworthy,
 making wise the simple.
[8]The precepts of the LORD are right,
 giving joy to the heart.
The commands of the LORD are radiant,
 giving light to the eyes.
[9]The fear of the LORD is pure,
 enduring forever.
The ordinances of the LORD are sure
 and altogether righteous.
[10]They are more precious than gold,
 than much pure gold;
they are sweeter than honey,
 than honey from the comb.
[11]By them is your servant warned;
 in keeping them there is great reward.

[12]Who can discern his errors?

[a] 3 Or *They have no speech, there are no words;* / *no sound is heard
from them*
[b] 4 Septuagint, Jerome and Syriac; Hebrew *line*

Forgive my hidden faults.
¹³Keep your servant also from willful sins;
  may they not rule over me.
Then will I be blameless,
  innocent of great transgression.

¹⁴May the words of my mouth and the meditation
    of my heart
  be pleasing in your sight,
  O LORD, my Rock and my Redeemer.

Psalm 20

For the director of music. A psalm of David.

¹May the LORD answer you when you are in
    distress;
  may the name of the God of Jacob protect you.
²May he send you help from the sanctuary
  and grant you support from Zion.
³May he remember all your sacrifices
  and accept your burnt offerings.   *Selah*
⁴May he give you the desire of your heart
  and make all your plans succeed.
⁵We will shout for joy when you are victorious
  and will lift up our banners in the name of our
    God.

May the LORD grant all your requests.

⁶Now I know that the LORD saves his anointed;
  he answers him from his holy heaven
  with the saving power of his right hand.
⁷Some trust in chariots and some in horses,
  but we trust in the name of the LORD our God.
⁸They are brought to their knees and fall,
  but we rise up and stand firm.

⁹O LORD, save the king!
  Answerᵃ us when we call!

ᵃ 9 Or *save! / O King, answer*

Psalm 21

For the director of music. A psalm of David.

¹O Lord, the king rejoices in your strength.
How great is his joy in the victories you give!
²You have granted him the desire of his heart
and have not withheld the request of his lips.
Selah

³You welcomed him with rich blessings
and placed a crown of pure gold on his head.
⁴He asked you for life, and you gave it to him—
length of days, for ever and ever.
⁵Through the victories you gave, his glory is great;
you have bestowed on him splendor and
majesty.
⁶Surely you have granted him eternal blessings
and made him glad with the joy of your
presence.
⁷For the king trusts in the Lord;
through the unfailing love of the Most High
he will not be shaken.

⁸Your hand will lay hold on all your enemies;
your right hand will seize your foes.
⁹At the time of your appearing
you will make them like a fiery furnace.
In his wrath the Lord will swallow them up,
and his fire will consume them.
¹⁰You will destroy their descendants from the earth,
their posterity from mankind.
¹¹Though they plot evil against you
and devise wicked schemes, they cannot
succeed;
¹²for you will make them turn their backs
when you aim at them with drawn bow.

¹³Be exalted, O Lord, in your strength;
we will sing and praise your might.

Psalm 22

For the director of music. To the tune of "The Doe of the Morning." A psalm of David.

¹My God, my God, why have you forsaken me?
  Why are you so far from saving me,
    so far from the words of my groaning?
²O my God, I cry out by day, but you do not
      answer,
  by night, and am not silent.

³Yet you are enthroned as the Holy One;
  you are the praise of Israel.ᵃ
⁴In you our fathers put their trust;
  they trusted and you delivered them.
⁵They cried to you and were saved;
  in you they trusted and were not disappointed.

⁶But I am a worm and not a man,
  scorned by men and despised by the people.
⁷All who see me mock me;
  they hurl insults, shaking their heads:
⁸"He trusts in the LORD;
  let the LORD rescue him.
Let him deliver him,
  since he delights in him."

⁹Yet you brought me out of the womb;
  you made me trust in you
    even at my mother's breast.
¹⁰From birth I was cast upon you;
  from my mother's womb you have been my
      God.
¹¹Do not be far from me,
  for trouble is near
  and there is no one to help.

¹²Many bulls surround me;
  strong bulls of Bashan encircle me.
¹³Roaring lions tearing their prey
  open their mouths wide against me.
¹⁴I am poured out like water,

ᵃ3 Or Yet you are holy, / enthroned on the praises of Israel

and all my bones are out of joint.
My heart has turned to wax;
  it has melted away within me.
¹⁵My strength is dried up like a potsherd,
  and my tongue sticks to the roof of my mouth;
  you lay me[a] in the dust of death.
¹⁶Dogs have surrounded me;
  a band of evil men has encircled me,
  they have pierced[b] my hands and my feet.
¹⁷I can count all my bones;
  people stare and gloat over me.
¹⁸They divide my garments among them
  and cast lots for my clothing.

¹⁹But you, O LORD, be not far off;
  O my Strength, come quickly to help me.
²⁰Deliver my life from the sword,
  my precious life from the power of the dogs.
²¹Rescue me from the mouth of the lions;
  save[c] me from the horns of the wild oxen.

²²I will declare your name to my brothers;
  in the congregation I will praise you.
²³You who fear the LORD, praise him!
  All you descendants of Jacob, honor him!
  Revere him, all you descendants of Israel!
²⁴For he has not despised or disdained
  the suffering of the afflicted one;
he has not hidden his face from him
  but has listened to his cry for help.

²⁵From you comes my praise in the great assembly;
  before those who fear you[d] will I fulfill my
    vows.
²⁶The poor will eat and be satisfied;
  they who seek the LORD will praise him—
  may your hearts live forever!
²⁷All the ends of the earth
  will remember and turn to the LORD,

a 15 Or / I am laid
b 16 Some Hebrew manuscripts, Septuagint and Syriac; most
Hebrew manuscripts / like the lion,
c 21 Or lions; / you have heard   d 25 Hebrew him

and all the families of the nations
  will bow down before him,
[28]for dominion belongs to the LORD
  and he rules over the nations.

[29]All the rich of the earth will feast and worship;
  all who go down to the dust will kneel before
      him—
  those who cannot keep themselves alive.
[30]Posterity will serve him;
  future generations will be told about the Lord.
[31]They will proclaim his righteousness
  to a people yet unborn—
  for he has done it.

Psalm 23

A psalm of David.

[1]The LORD is my shepherd, I shall lack nothing.
[2] He makes me lie down in green pastures,
he leads me beside quiet waters,
[3] he restores my soul.
He guides me in paths of righteousness
  for his name's sake.
[4]Even though I walk
  through the valley of the shadow of death,[a]
I will fear no evil,
  for you are with me;
your rod and your staff,
  they comfort me.

[5]You prepare a table before me
  in the presence of my enemies.
You anoint my head with oil;
  my cup overflows.
[6]Surely goodness and love will follow me
  all the days of my life,
and I will dwell in the house of the LORD
  forever.

[a] 4 Or *through the darkest valley*

Psalm 24

Of David. A psalm.

¹The earth is the LORD's, and everything in it,
    the world, and all who live in it;
²for he founded it upon the seas
    and established it upon the waters.

³Who may ascend the hill of the LORD?
    Who may stand in his holy place?
⁴He who has clean hands and a pure heart,
    who does not lift up his soul to an idol
    or swear by what is false.
⁵He will receive blessing from the LORD
    and vindication from God his Savior.
⁶Such is the generation of those who seek him,
    who seek your face, O God of Jacob.ᵃ   *Selah*

⁷Lift up your heads, O you gates;
    be lifted up, you ancient doors,
    that the King of glory may come in.
⁸Who is this King of glory?
    The LORD strong and mighty,
    the LORD mighty in battle.
⁹Lift up your heads, O you gates;
    lift them up, you ancient doors,
    that the King of glory may come in.
¹⁰Who is he, this King of glory?
    The LORD Almighty—
    he is the King of glory.   *Selah*

Psalm 25ᵇ

Of David.

¹To you, O LORD, I lift up my soul;
²   in you I trust, O my God.
 Do not let me be put to shame,
    nor let my enemies triumph over me.
³No one whose hope is in you

ᵃ6 Two Hebrew manuscripts and Syriac (see also Septuagint);
most Hebrew manuscripts *face, Jacob*
ᵇThis psalm is an acrostic poem, the verses of which begin with
the successive letters of the Hebrew alphabet.

will ever be put to shame,
but they will be put to shame
who are treacherous without excuse.

⁴Show me your ways, O LORD,
teach me your paths;
⁵guide me in your truth and teach me,
for you are God my Savior,
and my hope is in you all day long.
⁶Remember, O LORD, your great mercy and love,
for they are from of old.
⁷Remember not the sins of my youth
and my rebellious ways;
according to your love remember me,
for you are good, O LORD.

⁸Good and upright is the LORD;
therefore he instructs sinners in his ways.
⁹He guides the humble in what is right
and teaches them his way.
¹⁰All the ways of the LORD are loving and faithful
for those who keep the demands of his
covenant.
¹¹For the sake of your name, O LORD,
forgive my iniquity, though it is great.
¹²Who, then, is the man that fears the LORD?
He will instruct him in the way chosen for him.
¹³He will spend his days in prosperity,
and his descendants will inherit the land.
¹⁴The LORD confides in those who fear him;
he makes his covenant known to them.
¹⁵My eyes are ever on the LORD,
for only he will release my feet from the snare.

¹⁶Turn to me and be gracious to me,
for I am lonely and afflicted.
¹⁷The troubles of my heart have multiplied;
free me from my anguish.
¹⁸Look upon my affliction and my distress
and take away all my sins.
¹⁹See how my enemies have increased
and how fiercely they hate me!
²⁰Guard my life and rescue me;

let me not be put to shame,
for I take refuge in you.
²¹May integrity and uprightness protect me,
because my hope is in you.

²²Redeem Israel, O God,
from all their troubles!

Psalm 26

Of David.

¹Vindicate me, O LORD,
for I have led a blameless life;
I have trusted in the LORD
without wavering.
²Test me, O LORD, and try me,
examine my heart and my mind;
³for your love is ever before me,
and I walk continually in your truth.
⁴I do not sit with deceitful men,
nor do I consort with hypocrites;
⁵I abhor the assembly of evildoers
and refuse to sit with the wicked.
⁶I wash my hands in innocence,
and go about your altar, O LORD,
⁷proclaiming aloud your praise
and telling of all your wonderful deeds.
⁸I love the house where you live, O LORD,
the place where your glory dwells.

⁹Do not take away my soul along with sinners
or my life with bloodthirsty men,
¹⁰in whose hands are wicked schemes,
whose right hands are full of bribes.
¹¹But I lead a blameless life;
redeem me and be merciful to me.

¹²My feet stand on level ground;
in the great assembly I will praise the LORD.

Psalm 27

Of David.

[1]The LORD is my light and my salvation—
  whom shall I fear?
The LORD is the stronghold of my life—
  of whom shall I be afraid?
[2]When evil men advance against me
  to devour my flesh,[a]
when my enemies and my foes attack me,
  they will stumble and fall.
[3]Though an army besiege me,
  my heart will not fear;
though war break out against me,
  even then will I be confident.

[4]One thing I ask of the LORD,
  this is what I seek:
that I may dwell in the house of the LORD
  all the days of my life,
to gaze upon the beauty of the LORD
  and to seek him in his temple.
[5]For in the day of trouble
  he will keep me safe in his dwelling;
he will hide me in the shelter of his tabernacle
  and set me high upon a rock.
[6]Then my head will be exalted
  above the enemies who surround me;
at his tabernacle will I sacrifice with shouts of joy;
  I will sing and make music to the LORD.

[7]Hear my voice when I call, O LORD;
  be merciful to me and answer me.
[8]My heart says of you, "Seek his[b] face!"
  Your face, LORD, I will seek.
[9]Do not hide your face from me,
  do not turn your servant away in anger;
  you have been my helper.
Do not reject me or forsake me,
  O God my Savior.

[a] 2 Or *to slander me*
[b] 8 Or *To you, O my heart, he has said, "Seek my*

¹⁰Though my father and mother forsake me,
　　the LORD will receive me.
¹¹Teach me your way, O LORD;
　　lead me in a straight path
　　because of my oppressors.
¹²Do not turn me over to the desire of my foes,
　　for false witnesses rise up against me,
　　breathing out violence.

¹³I am still confident of this:
　　I will see the goodness of the LORD
　　in the land of the living.
¹⁴Wait for the LORD;
　　be strong and take heart
　　and wait for the LORD.

Psalm 28

Of David.

¹To you I call, O LORD my Rock;
　　do not turn a deaf ear to me.
　For if you remain silent,
　　I will be like those who have gone down to
　　　the pit.
²Hear my cry for mercy
　　as I call to you for help,
　as I lift up my hands
　　toward your Most Holy Place.

³Do not drag me away with the wicked,
　　with those who do evil,
　who speak cordially with their neighbors
　　but harbor malice in their hearts.
⁴Repay them for their deeds
　　and for their evil work;
　repay them for what their hands have done
　　and bring back upon them what they deserve.
⁵Since they show no regard for the works of the
　　LORD
　　and what his hands have done,
　he will tear them down
　　and never build them up again.

⁶Praise be to the LORD,
    for he has heard my cry for mercy.
⁷The LORD is my strength and my shield;
    my heart trusts in him, and I am helped.
My heart leaps for joy
    and I will give thanks to him in song.

⁸The LORD is the strength of his people,
    a fortress of salvation for his anointed one.
⁹Save your people and bless your inheritance;
    be their shepherd and carry them forever.

Psalm 29

A psalm of David.

¹Ascribe to the LORD, O mighty ones,
    ascribe to the LORD glory and strength.
²Ascribe to the LORD the glory due his name;
    worship the LORD in the splendor of his[a]
        holiness.

³The voice of the LORD is over the waters;
    the God of glory thunders,
    the LORD thunders over the mighty waters.
⁴The voice of the LORD is powerful;
    the voice of the LORD is majestic.
⁵The voice of the LORD breaks the cedars;
    the LORD breaks in pieces the cedars of
        Lebanon.
⁶He makes Lebanon skip like a calf,
    Sirion[b] like a young wild ox.
⁷The voice of the LORD strikes
    with flashes of lightning.
⁸The voice of the LORD shakes the desert;
    the LORD shakes the Desert of Kadesh.
⁹The voice of the LORD twists the oaks[c]
    and strips the forests bare.
And in his temple all cry, "Glory!"

¹⁰The LORD sits[d] enthroned over the flood;
    the LORD is enthroned as King forever.

---

a 2 Or LORD with the splendor of   b 6 That is, Mount Hermon
c 9 Or LORD makes the deer give birth   d 10 Or sat

¹¹The LORD gives strength to his people;
    the LORD blesses his people with peace.

Psalm 30

A psalm. A song. For the dedication of the temple.^a Of David.

¹I will exalt you, O LORD,
    for you lifted me out of the depths
    and did not let my enemies gloat over me.
²O LORD my God, I called to you for help
    and you healed me.
³O LORD, you brought me up from the grave^b;
    you spared me from going down into the pit.

⁴Sing to the LORD, you saints of his;
    praise his holy name.
⁵For his anger lasts only a moment,
    but his favor lasts a lifetime;
weeping may remain for a night,
    but rejoicing comes in the morning.

⁶When I felt secure, I said,
    "I will never be shaken."
⁷O LORD, when you favored me,
    you made my mountain^c stand firm;
but when you hid your face,
    I was dismayed.

⁸To you, O LORD, I called;
    to the Lord I cried for mercy:
⁹"What gain is there in my destruction,^d
    if I go down into the pit?
Will the dust praise you?
    Will it proclaim your faithfulness?
¹⁰Hear, O LORD, and be merciful to me;
    O LORD, be my help."

¹¹You turned my wailing into dancing;
    you removed my sackcloth and clothed me with
        joy,
¹²that my heart may sing to you and not be silent.
    O LORD my God, I will give you thanks forever.

---

^aTitle: Or *palace*   ^b3 Hebrew *Sheol*   ^c7 Or *hill country*
^d9 Or *there if I am silenced*

Psalm 31

For the director of music. A psalm of David.

¹In you, O LORD, I have taken refuge;
    let me never be put to shame;
    deliver me in your righteousness.
²Turn your ear to me,
    come quickly to my rescue;
  be my rock of refuge,
    a strong fortress to save me.
³Since you are my rock and my fortress,
    for the sake of your name lead and guide me.
⁴Free me from the trap that is set for me,
    for you are my refuge.
⁵Into your hands I commit my spirit;
    redeem me, O LORD, the God of truth.

⁶I hate those who cling to worthless idols;
    I trust in the LORD.
⁷I will be glad and rejoice in your love,
    for you saw my affliction
    and knew the anguish of my soul.
⁸You have not handed me over to the enemy
    but have set my feet in a spacious place.

⁹Be merciful to me, O LORD, for I am in distress;
    my eyes grow weak with sorrow,
    my soul and my body with grief.
¹⁰My life is consumed by anguish
    and my years by groaning;
  my strength fails because of my affliction,ᵃ
    and my bones grow weak.
¹¹Because of all my enemies,
    I am the utter contempt of my neighbors;
  I am a dread to my friends—
    those who see me on the street flee from me.
¹²I am forgotten by them as though I were dead;
    I have become like broken pottery.
¹³For I hear the slander of many;

ᵃ 10 Or *guilt*

there is terror on every side;
they conspire against me
and plot to take my life.

14But I trust in you, O Lord;
    I say, "You are my God."
15My times are in your hands;
    deliver me from my enemies
    and from those who pursue me.
16Let your face shine on your servant;
    save me in your unfailing love.
17Let me not be put to shame, O Lord,
    for I have cried out to you;
but let the wicked be put to shame
    and lie silent in the grave.a
18Let their lying lips be silenced,
    for with pride and contempt
    they speak arrogantly against the righteous.

19How great is your goodness,
    which you have stored up for those who fear
        you,
    which you bestow in the sight of men
    on those who take refuge in you.
20In the shelter of your presence you hide them
    from the intrigues of men;
in your dwelling you keep them safe
    from the strife of tongues.

21Praise be to the Lord,
    for he showed his wonderful love to me
    when I was in a besieged city.
22In my alarm I said,
    "I am cut off from your sight!"
Yet you heard my cry for mercy
    when I called to you for help.

23Love the Lord, all his saints!
    The Lord preserves the faithful,
    but the proud he pays back in full.
24Be strong and take heart,
    all you who hope in the Lord.

a 17 Hebrew *Sheol*

Psalm 32

Of David. A *maskil.*[a]

[1]Blessed is he
    whose transgressions are forgiven,
    whose sins are covered.
[2]Blessed is the man
    whose sin the Lord does not count against him
    and in whose spirit is no deceit.

[3]When I kept silent,
    my bones wasted away
    through my groaning all day long.
[4]For day and night
    your hand was heavy upon me;
my strength was sapped
    as in the heat of summer.   *Selah*
[5]Then I acknowledged my sin to you
    and did not cover up my iniquity.
I said, "I will confess
    my transgressions to the Lord"—
and you forgave
    the guilt of my sin.   *Selah*

[6]Therefore let everyone who is godly pray to you
    while you may be found;
surely when the mighty waters rise,
    they will not reach him.
[7]You are my hiding place;
    you will protect me from trouble
    and surround me with songs of deliverance.
        Selah

[8]I will instruct you and teach you in the way you
        should go;
    I will counsel you and watch over you.
[9]Do not be like the horse or the mule,
    which have no understanding
but must be controlled by bit and bridle
    or they will not come to you.
[10]Many are the woes of the wicked,

---

[a] Title: Probably a literary or musical term

but the LORD's unfailing love
surrounds the man who trusts in him.

[11]Rejoice in the LORD and be glad, you righteous;
sing, all you who are upright in heart!

Psalm 33

[1]Sing joyfully to the LORD, you righteous;
it is fitting for the upright to praise him.
[2]Praise the LORD with the harp;
make music to him on the ten-stringed lyre.
[3]Sing to him a new song;
play skillfully, and shout for joy.

[4]For the word of the LORD is right and true;
he is faithful in all he does.
[5]The LORD loves righteousness and justice;
the earth is full of his unfailing love.

[6]By the word of the LORD were the heavens made,
their starry host by the breath of his mouth.
[7]He gathers the waters of the sea into jars[a];
he puts the deep into storehouses.
[8]Let all the earth fear the LORD;
let all the people of the world revere him.
[9]For he spoke, and it came to be;
he commanded, and it stood firm.
[10]The LORD foils the plans of the nations;
he thwarts the purposes of the peoples.
[11]But the plans of the LORD stand firm forever,
the purposes of his heart through all
generations.

[12]Blessed is the nation whose God is the LORD,
the people he chose for his inheritance.
[13]From heaven the LORD looks down
and sees all mankind;
[14]from his dwelling place he watches
all who live on earth—
[15]he who forms the hearts of all,
who considers everything they do.

[a]7 Or *sea as into a heap*

[16]No king is saved by the size of his army;
  no warrior escapes by his great strength.
[17]A horse is a vain hope for deliverance;
  despite all its great strength it cannot save.
[18]But the eyes of the LORD are on those who fear
    him,
  on those whose hope is in his unfailing love,
[19]to deliver them from death
  and keep them alive in famine.

[20]We wait in hope for the LORD;
  he is our help and our shield.
[21]In him our hearts rejoice,
  for we trust in his holy name.
[22]May your unfailing love rest upon us, O LORD,
  even as we put our hope in you.

Psalm 34[a]

Of David. When he feigned insanity before Abimelech, who drove
him away, and he left.

[1]I will extol the LORD at all times;
  his praise will always be on my lips.
[2]My soul will boast in the LORD;
  let the afflicted hear and rejoice.
[3]Glorify the LORD with me;
  let us exalt his name together.

[4]I sought the LORD, and he answered me;
  he delivered me from all my fears.
[5]Those who look to him are radiant;
  their faces are never covered with shame.
[6]This poor man called, and the LORD heard him;
  he saved him out of all his troubles.
[7]The angel of the LORD encamps around those who
    fear him,
  and he delivers them.

[8]Taste and see that the LORD is good;
  blessed is the man who takes refuge in him.
[9]Fear the LORD, you his saints,

[a]This psalm is an acrostic poem, the verses of which begin with
the successive letters of the Hebrew alphabet.

for those who fear him lack nothing.
10The lions may grow weak and hungry,
   but those who seek the LORD lack no good
      thing.

11Come, my children, listen to me;
   I will teach you the fear of the LORD.
12Whoever of you loves life
   and desires to see many good days,
13keep your tongue from evil
   and your lips from speaking lies.
14Turn from evil and do good;
   seek peace and pursue it.

15The eyes of the LORD are on the righteous
   and his ears are attentive to their cry;
16the face of the LORD is against those who do evil,
   to cut off the memory of them from the earth.

17The righteous cry out, and the LORD hears them;
   he delivers them from all their troubles.
18The LORD is close to the brokenhearted
   and saves those who are crushed in spirit.

19A righteous man may have many troubles,
   but the LORD delivers him from them all;
20he protects all his bones,
   not one of them will be broken.

21Evil will slay the wicked;
   the foes of the righteous will be condemned.
22The LORD redeems his servants;
   no one who takes refuge in him will be
      condemned.

Psalm 35

Of David.

1Contend, O LORD, with those who contend with
      me;
   fight against those who fight against me.
2Take up shield and buckler;
   arise and come to my aid.

³Brandish spear and javelinᵃ
    against those who pursue me.
Say to my soul,
    "I am your salvation."

⁴May those who seek my life
    be disgraced and put to shame;
may those who plot my ruin
    be turned back in dismay.
⁵May they be like chaff before the wind,
    with the angel of the LORD driving them away;
⁶may their path be dark and slippery,
    with the angel of the LORD pursuing them.
⁷Since they hid their net for me without cause
    and without cause dug a pit for me,
⁸may ruin overtake them by surprise—
    may the net they hid entangle them,
    may they fall into the pit, to their ruin.
⁹Then my soul will rejoice in the LORD
    and delight in his salvation.
¹⁰My whole being will exclaim,
    "Who is like you, O LORD?
You rescue the poor from those too strong for
        them,
    the poor and needy from those who rob them."

¹¹Ruthless witnesses come forward;
    they question me on things I know nothing
        about.
¹²They repay me evil for good
    and leave my soul forlorn.
¹³Yet when they were ill, I put on sackcloth
    and humbled myself with fasting.
When my prayers returned to me unanswered,
¹⁴   I went about mourning
    as though for my friend or brother.
I bowed my head in grief
    as though weeping for my mother.
¹⁵But when I stumbled, they gathered in glee;
    attackers gathered against me when I was
        unaware.

ᵃ 3 Or *and block the way*

They slandered me without ceasing.
[16]Like the ungodly they maliciously mocked[a];
  they gnashed their teeth at me.

[17]O LORD, how long will you look on?
  Rescue my life from their ravages,
  my precious life from these lions.
[18]I will give you thanks in the great assembly;
  among throngs of people I will praise you.
[19]Let not those gloat over me
  who are my enemies without cause;
 let not those who hate me without reason
  maliciously wink the eye.
[20]They do not speak peaceably,
  but devise false accusations
  against those who live quietly in the land.
[21]They gape at me and say, "Aha! Aha!
  With our own eyes we have seen it."

[22]O LORD, you have seen this; be not silent.
  Do not be far from me, O Lord.
[23]Awake, and rise to my defense!
  Contend for me, my God and Lord.
[24]Vindicate me in your righteousness, O LORD my
    God;
  do not let them gloat over me.
[25]Do not let them think, "Aha, just what we
    wanted!"
  or say, "We have swallowed him up."

[26]May all who gloat over my distress
  be put to shame and confusion;
 may all who exalt themselves over me
  be clothed with shame and disgrace.
[27]May those who delight in my vindication
  shout for joy and gladness;
 may they always say, "The LORD be exalted,
  who delights in the well-being of his servant."
[28]My tongue will speak of your righteousness
  and of your praises all day long.

[a] 16 Septuagint; Hebrew may mean *ungodly circle of mockers.*

Psalm 36

For the director of music. Of David the servant of the LORD.

[1]An oracle is within my heart
  concerning the sinfulness of the wicked:[a]
There is no fear of God
  before his eyes.
[2]For in his own eyes he flatters himself
  too much to detect or hate his sin.
[3]The words of his mouth are wicked and deceitful;
  he has ceased to be wise and to do good.
[4]Even on his bed he plots evil;
  he commits himself to a sinful course
  and does not reject what is wrong.

[5]Your love, O LORD, reaches to the heavens,
  your faithfulness to the skies.
[6]Your righteousness is like the mighty mountains,
  your justice like the great deep.
O LORD, you preserve both man and beast.
[7] How priceless is your unfailing love!
Both high and low among men
  find[b] refuge in the shadow of your wings.
[8]They feast on the abundance of your house;
  you give them drink from your river of
      delights.
[9]For with you is the fountain of life;
  in your light we see light.

[10]Continue your love to those who know you,
  your righteousness to the upright in heart.
[11]May the foot of the proud not come against me,
  nor the hand of the wicked drive me away.
[12]See how the evildoers lie fallen—
  thrown down, not able to rise!

[a]1 Or heart: / Sin proceeds from the wicked.
[b]7 Or love, O God! / Men find; or love! / Both heavenly beings and
men / find

Psalm 37[a]

Of David.

[1]Do not fret because of evil men
    or be envious of those who do wrong;
[2]for like the grass they will soon wither,
    like green plants they will soon die away.

[3]Trust in the LORD and do good;
    dwell in the land and enjoy safe pasture.
[4]Delight yourself in the LORD
    and he will give you the desires of your heart.

[5]Commit your way to the LORD;
    trust in him and he will do this:
[6]He will make your righteousness shine like the
        dawn,
    the justice of your cause like the noonday sun.

[7]Be still before the LORD and wait patiently for him;
    do not fret when men succeed in their ways,
    when they carry out their wicked schemes.

[8]Refrain from anger and turn from wrath;
    do not fret—it leads only to evil.
[9]For evil men will be cut off,
    but those who hope in the LORD will inherit the
        land.

[10]A little while, and the wicked will be no more;
    though you look for them, they will not be
        found.
[11]But the meek will inherit the land
    and enjoy great peace.

[12]The wicked plot against the righteous
    and gnash their teeth at them;
[13]but the Lord laughs at the wicked,
    for he knows their day is coming.

[14]The wicked draw the sword
    and bend the bow

---

[a] This psalm is an acrostic poem, the stanzas of which begin with
the successive letters of the Hebrew alphabet.

to bring down the poor and needy,
to slay those whose ways are upright.
¹⁵But their swords will pierce their own hearts,
and their bows will be broken.

¹⁶Better the little that the righteous have
than the wealth of many wicked;
¹⁷for the power of the wicked will be broken,
but the LORD upholds the righteous.

¹⁸The days of the blameless are known to the LORD,
and their inheritance will endure forever.
¹⁹In times of disaster they will not wither;
in days of famine they will enjoy plenty.

²⁰But the wicked will perish:
The LORD's enemies will be like the beauty of
the fields,
they will vanish—vanish like smoke.

²¹The wicked borrow and do not repay,
but the righteous give generously;
²²those the LORD blesses will inherit the land,
but those he curses will be cut off.

²³The LORD delights in the way of the man
whose steps he has made firm;
²⁴though he stumble, he will not fall,
for the LORD upholds him with his hand.

²⁵I was young and now I am old,
yet I have never seen the righteous forsaken
or their children begging bread.
²⁶They are always generous and lend freely;
their children will be blessed.

²⁷Turn from evil and do good;
then you will always live securely.
²⁸For the LORD loves the just
and will not forsake his faithful ones.

They will be protected forever,
but the offspring of the wicked will be cut off;
²⁹the righteous will inherit the land
and dwell in it forever.

30The mouth of the righteous man utters wisdom,
    and his tongue speaks what is just.
31The law of his God is in his heart;
    his feet do not slip.

32The wicked lie in wait for the righteous,
    seeking their very lives;
33but the LORD will not leave them in their power
    or let them be condemned when brought to
        trial.

34Wait for the LORD
    and keep his way.
  He will exalt you to possess the land;
    when the wicked are cut off, you will see it.

35I have seen a wicked and ruthless man
    flourishing like a green tree in its native soil,
36but he soon passed away and was no more;
    though I looked for him, he could not be found.

37Consider the blameless, observe the upright;
    there is a future[a] for the man of peace.
38But all sinners will be destroyed;
    the future[b] of the wicked will be cut off.

39The salvation of the righteous comes from the
        LORD;
    he is their stronghold in time of trouble.
40The LORD helps them and delivers them;
    he delivers them from the wicked and saves
        them,
    because they take refuge in him.

Psalm 38

A psalm of David. A petition.

1O LORD, do not rebuke me in your anger
    or discipline me in your wrath.
2For your arrows have pierced me,
    and your hand has come down upon me.

a 37 Or *there will be posterity*   b 38 Or *posterity*

[3]Because of your wrath there is no health in my
        body;
    my bones have no soundness because of
        my sin.
[4]My guilt has overwhelmed me
    like a burden too heavy to bear.

[5]My wounds fester and are loathsome
    because of my sinful folly.
[6]I am bowed down and brought very low;
    all day long I go about mourning.
[7]My back is filled with searing pain;
    there is no health in my body.
[8]I am feeble and utterly crushed;
    I groan in anguish of heart.

[9]All my longings lie open before you, O Lord;
    my sighing is not hidden from you.
[10]My heart pounds, my strength fails me;
    even the light has gone from my eyes.
[11]My friends and companions avoid me because of
        my wounds;
    my neighbors stay far away.
[12]Those who seek my life set their traps,
    those who would harm me talk of my ruin;
    all day long they plot deception.

[13]I am like a deaf man, who cannot hear,
    like a mute, who cannot open his mouth;
[14]I have become like a man who does not hear,
    whose mouth can offer no reply.
[15]I wait for you, O LORD;
    you will answer, O Lord my God.
[16]For I said, "Do not let them gloat
    or exalt themselves over me when my foot
        slips."

[17]For I am about to fall,
    and my pain is ever with me.
[18]I confess my iniquity;
    I am troubled by my sin.
[19]Many are those who are my vigorous enemies;

those who hate me without reason are
   numerous.
²⁰Those who repay my good with evil
   slander me when I seek what is good.

²¹O LORD, do not forsake me;
   be not far from me, O my God.
²²Come quickly to help me,
   O Lord my Savior.

Psalm 39

For the director of music. For Jeduthun. A psalm of David.

¹I said, "I will watch my ways
   and keep my tongue from sin;
 I will put a muzzle on my mouth
   as long as the wicked are in my presence."
²But when I was silent and still,
   not even saying anything good,
   my anguish increased.
³My heart grew hot within me,
   and as I meditated, the fire burned;
   then I spoke with my tongue:

⁴"Show me, O LORD, my life's end
   and the number of my days;
   let me know how fleeting is my life.
⁵You have made my days a mere handbreadth;
   the span of my years is as nothing before you.
   Each man's life is but a breath.   *Selah*
⁶Man is a mere phantom as he goes to and fro:
   He bustles about, but only in vain;
   he heaps up wealth, not knowing who will
      get it.

⁷"But now, Lord, what do I look for?
   My hope is in you.
⁸Save me from all my transgressions;
   do not make me the scorn of fools.
⁹I was silent; I would not open my mouth,
   for you are the one who has done this.
¹⁰Remove your scourge from me;
   I am overcome by the blow of your hand.

¹¹You rebuke and discipline men for their sin;
  you consume their wealth like a moth—
  each man is but a breath.   *Selah*

¹²"Hear my prayer, O LORD,
  listen to my cry for help;
  be not deaf to my weeping.
For I dwell with you as an alien,
  a stranger, as all my fathers were.
¹³Look away from me, that I may rejoice again
  before I depart and am no more."

Psalm 40

For the director of music. Of David. A psalm.

¹I waited patiently for the LORD;
  he turned to me and heard my cry.
²He lifted me out of the slimy pit,
  out of the mud and mire;
he set my feet on a rock
  and gave me a firm place to stand.
³He put a new song in my mouth,
  a hymn of praise to our God.
Many will see and fear
  and put their trust in the LORD.

⁴Blessed is the man
  who makes the LORD his trust,
who does not look to the proud,
  to those who turn aside to false gods.^a
⁵Many, O LORD my God,
  are the wonders you have done.
The things you planned for us
  no one can recount to you;
were I to speak and tell of them,
  they would be too many to declare.

⁶Sacrifice and offering you did not desire,
  but my ears you have pierced^{b, c};

---

^a4 Or *to falsehood*
^b6 Hebrew; Septuagint *but a body you have prepared for me* (see also
Symmachus and Theodotion)
^c6 Or *opened*

burnt offerings and sin offerings
  you did not require.
[7]Then I said, "Here I am, I have come—
  it is written about me in the scroll.[a]
[8]To do your will, O my God, is my desire;
  your law is within my heart."

[9]I proclaim righteousness in the great assembly;
  I do not seal my lips,
  as you know, O Lord.
[10]I do not hide your righteousness in my heart;
  I speak of your faithfulness and salvation.
I do not conceal your love and your truth
  from the great assembly.

[11]Do not withhold your mercy from me, O Lord;
  may your love and your truth always protect
    me.
[12]For troubles without number surround me;
  my sins have overtaken me, and I cannot see.
They are more than the hairs of my head,
  and my heart fails within me.

[13]Be pleased, O Lord, to save me;
  O Lord, come quickly to help me.
[14]May all who seek to take my life
  be put to shame and confusion;
may all who desire my ruin
  be turned back in disgrace.
[15]May those who say to me, "Aha! Aha!"
  be appalled at their own shame.
[16]But may all who seek you
  rejoice and be glad in you;
may those who love your salvation always say,
  "The Lord be exalted!"

[17]Yet I am poor and needy;
  may the Lord think of me.
You are my help and my deliverer;
  O my God, do not delay.

[a]7 Or *come / with the scroll written for me*

Psalm 41

For the director of music. A psalm of David.

¹Blessed is he who has regard for the weak;
    the LORD delivers him in times of trouble.
²The LORD will protect him and preserve his life;
    he will bless him in the land
    and not surrender him to the desire of his foes.
³The LORD will sustain him on his sickbed
    and restore him from his bed of illness.

⁴I said, "O LORD, have mercy on me;
    heal me, for I have sinned against you."
⁵My enemies say of me in malice,
    "When will he die and his name perish?"
⁶Whenever one comes to see me,
    he speaks falsely, while his heart gathers
        slander;
    then he goes out and spreads it abroad.

⁷All my enemies whisper together against me;
    they imagine the worst for me, saying,
⁸"A vile disease has beset him;
    he will never get up from the place where he
        lies."
⁹Even my close friend, whom I trusted,
    he who shared my bread,
    has lifted up his heel against me.

¹⁰But you, O LORD, have mercy on me;
    raise me up, that I may repay them.
¹¹I know that you are pleased with me,
    for my enemy does not triumph over me.
¹²In my integrity you uphold me
    and set me in your presence forever.

¹³Praise be to the LORD, the God of Israel,
    from everlasting to everlasting.
            Amen and Amen.

BOOK II

Psalms 42-72

Psalm 42^a

For the director of music. A *maskil*^b of the Sons of Korah.

¹As the deer pants for streams of water,
   so my soul pants for you, O God.
²My soul thirsts for God, for the living God.
   When can I go and meet with God?
³My tears have been my
   food day and night,
while men say to me all day long,
   "Where is your God?"
⁴These things I remember
   as I pour out my soul:
how I used to go with the multitude,
   leading the procession to the house of God,
with shouts of joy and thanksgiving
  among the festive throng.

⁵Why are you downcast, O my soul?
   Why so disturbed within me?
Put your hope in God,
   for I will yet praise him,
   my Savior and ⁶my God.

My^c soul is downcast within me;
   therefore I will remember you
from the land of the Jordan,
   the heights of Hermon—from Mount Mizar.
⁷Deep calls to deep
   in the roar of your waterfalls;
all your waves and breakers
   have swept over me.

⁸By day the LORD directs his love,
   at night his song is with me—

^a In many Hebrew manuscripts Psalms 42 and 43 constitute one
psalm.
^b Title: Probably a literary or musical term
^c 5,6 A few Hebrew manuscripts, Septuagint and Syriac; most
Hebrew manuscripts *praise him for his saving help.* / ⁶*O my God, my*

a prayer to the God of my life.

[9]I say to God my Rock,
  "Why have you forgotten me?
Why must I go about mourning,
  oppressed by the enemy?"
[10]My bones suffer mortal agony
  as my foes taunt me,
saying to me all day long,
  "Where is your God?"

[11]Why are you downcast, O my soul?
  Why so disturbed within me?
Put your hope in God,
  for I will yet praise him,
  my Savior and my God.

Psalm 43[a]

[1]Vindicate me, O God,
  and plead my cause against an ungodly nation;
  rescue me from deceitful and wicked men.
[2]You are God my stronghold.
  Why have you rejected me?
Why must I go about mourning,
  oppressed by the enemy?
[3]Send forth your light and your truth,
  let them guide me;
let them bring me to your holy mountain,
  to the place where you dwell.
[4]Then will I go to the altar of God,
  to God, my joy and my delight.
I will praise you with the harp,
  O God, my God.

[5]Why are you downcast, O my soul?
  Why so disturbed within me?
Put your hope in God,
  for I will yet praise him,
  my Savior and my God.

[a]In many Hebrew manuscripts Psalms 42 and 43 constitute one psalm.

Psalm 44

For the director of music. Of the Sons of Korah. A *maskil.*[a]

¹We have heard with our ears, O God;
    our fathers have told us
what you did in their days,
    in days long ago.
²With your hand you drove out the nations
    and planted our fathers;
you crushed the peoples
    and made our fathers flourish.
³It was not by their sword that they won the land,
    nor did their arm bring them victory;
it was your right hand, your arm,
    and the light of your face, for you loved them.

⁴You are my King and my God,
    who decrees[b] victories for Jacob.
⁵Through you we push back our enemies;
    through your name we trample our foes.
⁶I do not trust in my bow,
    my sword does not bring me victory;
⁷but you give us victory over our enemies,
    you put our adversaries to shame.
⁸In God we make our boast all day long,
    and we will praise your name forever.   *Selah*

⁹But now you have rejected and humbled us;
    you no longer go out with our armies.
¹⁰You made us retreat before the enemy,
    and our adversaries have plundered us.
¹¹You gave us up to be devoured like sheep
    and have scattered us among the nations.
¹²You sold your people for a pittance,
    gaining nothing from their sale.

¹³You have made us a reproach to our neighbors,
    the scorn and derision of those around us.
¹⁴You have made us a byword among the nations;
    the peoples shake their heads at us.
¹⁵My disgrace is before me all day long,

---

^a Title: Probably a literary or musical term
^b 4 Septuagint, Aquila and Syriac; Hebrew *King, O God; / command*

and my face is covered with shame
16at the taunts of those who reproach and revile me,
   because of the enemy, who is bent on revenge.

17All this happened to us,
   though we had not forgotten you
   or been false to your covenant.
18Our hearts had not turned back;
   our feet had not strayed from your path.
19But you crushed us and made us a haunt for
      jackals
   and covered us over with deep darkness.

20If we had forgotten the name of our God
   or spread out our hands to a foreign god,
21would not God have discovered it,
   since he knows the secrets of the heart?
22Yet for your sake we face death all day long;
   we are considered as sheep to be slaughtered.

23Awake, O Lord! Why do you sleep?
   Rouse yourself! Do not reject us forever.
24Why do you hide your face
   and forget our misery and oppression?

25We are brought down to the dust;
   our bodies cling to the ground.
26Rise up and help us;
   redeem us because of your unfailing love.

Psalm 45

For the director of music. To the tune of "Lilies." Of the Sons of
Korah. A *maskil*.[a] A wedding song.

1My heart is stirred by a noble theme
   as I recite my verses for the king;
   my tongue is the pen of a skillful writer.

2You are the most excellent of men
   and your lips have been anointed with grace,
   since God has blessed you forever.
3Gird your sword upon your side, O mighty one;
   clothe yourself with splendor and majesty.

a Title: Probably a literary or musical term

⁴In your majesty ride forth victoriously
  in behalf of truth, humility and righteousness;
  let your right hand display awesome deeds.
⁵Let your sharp arrows pierce the hearts of the
        king's enemies;
  let the nations fall beneath your feet.
⁶Your throne, O God, will last for ever and ever;
  a scepter of justice will be the scepter of your
        kingdom.
⁷You love righteousness and hate wickedness;
  therefore God, your God, has set you above
        your companions
  by anointing you with the oil of joy.
⁸All your robes are fragrant with myrrh and aloes
        and cassia;
  from palaces adorned with ivory
  the music of the strings makes you glad.
⁹Daughters of kings are among your honored
        women;
  at your right hand is the royal bride in gold of
        Ophir.

¹⁰Listen, O daughter, consider and give ear:
  Forget your people and your father's house.
¹¹The king is enthralled by your beauty;
  honor him, for he is your lord.
¹²The Daughter of Tyre will come with a gift,ᵃ
  men of wealth will seek your favor.

¹³All glorious is the princess within her chamber;
  her gown is interwoven with gold.
¹⁴In embroidered garments she is led to the king;
  her virgin companions follow her
  and are brought to you.
¹⁵They are led in with joy and gladness;
  they enter the palace of the king.

¹⁶Your sons will take the place of your fathers;
  you will make them princes throughout the
        land.

ᵃ 12 Or *A Tyrian robe is among the gifts*

[17]I will perpetuate your memory through all
         generations;
    therefore the nations will praise you for ever
         and ever.

Psalm 46

For the director of music. Of the Sons of Korah. According to
                alamoth.[a] A song.

[1]God is our refuge and strength,
    an ever present help in trouble.
[2]Therefore we will not fear, though the earth give
         way
    and the mountains fall into the heart of the sea,
[3]though its waters roar and foam
    and the mountains quake with their surging.
                                                    Selah

[4]There is a river whose streams make glad the city
         of God,
    the holy place where the Most High dwells.
[5]God is within her, she will not fall;
    God will help her at break of day.
[6]Nations are in uproar, kingdoms fall;
    he lifts his voice, the earth melts.

[7]The LORD Almighty is with us;
    the God of Jacob is our fortress.   *Selah*

[8]Come and see the works of the LORD,
    the desolations he has brought on the earth.
[9]He makes wars cease to the ends of the earth;
    he breaks the bow and shatters the spear,
    he burns the shields[b] with fire.
[10]"Be still, and know that I am God;
    I will be exalted among the nations,
    I will be exalted in the earth."

[11]The LORD Almighty is with us;
    the God of Jacob is our fortress.   *Selah*

---

[a] Title: Probably a musical term   [b] 9 Or *chariots*

Psalm 47

For the director of music. Of the Sons of Korah. A psalm.

¹Clap your hands, all you nations;
    shout to God with cries of joy.
²How awesome is the LORD Most High,
    the great King over all the earth!
³He subdued nations under us,
    peoples under our feet.
⁴He chose our inheritance for us,
    the pride of Jacob, whom he loved.   *Selah*

⁵God has ascended amid shouts of joy,
    the LORD amid the sounding of trumpets.
⁶Sing praises to God, sing praises;
    sing praises to our King, sing praises.

⁷For God is the King of all the earth;
    sing to him a psalmᵃ of praise.
⁸God reigns over the nations;
    God is seated on his holy throne.
⁹The nobles of the nations assemble
    as the people of the God of Abraham,
for the kingsᵇ of the earth belong to God;
    he is greatly exalted.

Psalm 48

A song. A psalm of the Sons of Korah.

¹Great is the LORD, and most worthy of praise,
    in the city of our God, his holy mountain.
²It is beautiful in its loftiness,
    the joy of the whole earth.
Like the utmost heights of Zaphonᶜ is Mount
        Zion,
    theᵈ city of the Great King.
³God is in her citadels;
    he has shown himself to be her fortress.

ᵃ7 Or *a maskil* (probably a literary or musical term)
ᵇ9 Or *shields*
ᶜ2 *Zaphon* can refer to a sacred mountain or the direction north.
ᵈ2 Or *earth, / Mount Zion, on the northern side / of the*

⁴When the kings joined forces,
   when they advanced together,
⁵they saw her and were astounded;
   they fled in terror.
⁶Trembling seized them there,
   pain like that of a woman in labor.
⁷You destroyed them like ships of Tarshish
   shattered by an east wind.

⁸As we have heard,
   so have we seen
 in the city of the Lord Almighty,
   in the city of our God:
   God makes her secure forever.   *Selah*

⁹Within your temple, O God,
   we meditate on your unfailing love.
¹⁰Like your name, O God,
   your praise reaches to the ends of the earth;
   your right hand is filled with righteousness.
¹¹Mount Zion rejoices,
   the villages of Judah are glad
   because of your judgments.

¹²Walk about Zion, go around her,
   count her towers,
¹³consider well her ramparts,
   view her citadels,
   that you may tell of them to the next
      generation.
¹⁴For this God is our God for ever and ever;
   he will be our guide even to the end.

Psalm 49

For the director of music. Of the Sons of Korah. A psalm.

¹Hear this, all you peoples;
   listen, all who live in this world,
²both low and high,
   rich and poor alike:
³My mouth will speak words of wisdom;
   the utterance from my heart will give
      understanding.

⁴I will turn my ear to a proverb;
    with the harp I will expound my riddle:

⁵Why should I fear when evil days come,
    when wicked deceivers surround me—
⁶those who trust in their wealth
    and boast of their great riches?
⁷No man can redeem the life of another
    or give to God a ransom for him—
⁸the ransom for a life is costly,
    no payment is ever enough—
⁹that he should live on forever
    and not see decay.

¹⁰For all can see that wise men die;
    the foolish and the senseless alike perish
    and leave their wealth to others.
¹¹Their tombs will remain their housesᵃ forever,
    their dwellings for endless generations,
    though they hadᵇ named lands after themselves.

¹²But man, despite his riches, does not endure;
    he isᶜ like the beasts that perish.

¹³This is the fate of those who trust in themselves,
    and of their followers, who approve their
        sayings.   *Selah*
¹⁴Like sheep they are destined for the grave,ᵈ
    and death will feed on them.
The upright will rule over them in the morning;
    their forms will decay in the graveᵈ
    far from their princely mansions.
¹⁵But God will redeem my souleᵉ from the grave;
    he will surely take me to himself.   *Selah*

¹⁶Do not be overawed when a man grows rich,
    when the splendor of his house increases;
¹⁷for he will take nothing with him when he dies,
    his splendor will not descend with him.

ᵃ 11 Septuagint and Syriac; Hebrew *In their thoughts their houses
will be*   ᵇ 11 Or / *for they have*
ᶜ 12 Hebrew; Septuagint and Syriac *But a man who has riches
without understanding* / *is*
ᵈ 14 Hebrew *Sheol*; also in verse 15   ᵉ 15 Or *redeem me*

¹⁸Though while he lived he counted himself
        blessed—
    and men praise you when you prosper—
¹⁹he will join the generation of his fathers,
    who will never see the light ˌof lifeˌ.

²⁰A man who has riches without understanding
    is like the beasts that perish.

Psalm 50

A psalm of Asaph.

¹The Mighty One, God, the LORD,
    speaks and summons the earth
    from the rising of the sun to the place where
        it sets.
²From Zion, perfect in beauty,
    God shines forth.
³Our God comes and will not be silent;
    a fire devours before him,
    and around him a tempest rages.
⁴He summons the heavens above,
    and the earth, that he may judge his people:
⁵"Gather to me my consecrated ones,
    who made a covenant with me by sacrifice."
⁶And the heavens proclaim his righteousness,
    for God himself is judge.   Selah

⁷"Hear, O my people, and I will speak,
    O Israel, and I will testify against you:
    I am God, your God.
⁸I do not rebuke you for your sacrifices
    or your burnt offerings, which are ever
        before me.
⁹I have no need of a bull from your stall
    or of goats from your pens,
¹⁰for every animal of the forest is mine,
    and the cattle on a thousand hills.
¹¹I know every bird in the mountains,
    and the creatures of the field are mine.
¹²If I were hungry I would not tell you,
    for the world is mine, and all that is in it.

> 13Do I eat the flesh of bulls
>   or drink the blood of goats?
> 14Sacrifice thank offerings to God,
>   fulfill your vows to the Most High,
> 15and call upon me in the day of trouble;
>   I will deliver you, and you will honor me."

16But to the wicked, God says:

> "What right have you to recite my laws
>   or take my covenant on your lips?
> 17You hate my instruction
>   and cast my words behind you.
> 18When you see a thief, you join with him;
>   you throw in your lot with adulterers.
> 19You use your mouth for evil
>   and harness your tongue to deceit.
> 20You speak continually against your brother
>   and slander your own mother's son.
> 21These things you have done and I kept silent;
>   you thought I was altogether[a] like you.
> But I will rebuke you
>   and accuse you to your face.

> 22"Consider this, you who forget God,
>   or I will tear you to pieces, with none to rescue:
> 23He who sacrifices thank offerings honors me,
>   and he prepares the way
>   so that I may show him[b] the salvation of God."

Psalm 51

For the director of music. A psalm of David. When the prophet Nathan came to him after David had committed adultery with Bathsheba.

> 1Have mercy on me, O God,
>   according to your unfailing love;
> according to your great compassion
>   blot out my transgressions.
> 2Wash away all my iniquity
>   and cleanse me from my sin.

---

a 21 Or *thought the 'I AM' was*
b 23 Or *and to him who considers his way / I will show*

³For I know my transgressions,
   and my sin is always before me.
⁴Against you, you only, have I sinned
   and done what is evil in your sight,
so that you are proved right when you speak
   and justified when you judge.
⁵Surely I have been a sinner from birth,
   sinful from the time my mother conceived me.
⁶Surely you desire truth in the inner parts[a];
   you teach[b] me wisdom in the inmost place.

⁷Cleanse me with hyssop, and I will be clean;
   wash me, and I will be whiter than snow.
⁸Let me hear joy and gladness;
   let the bones you have crushed rejoice.
⁹Hide your face from my sins
   and blot out all my iniquity.

¹⁰Create in me a pure heart, O God,
   and renew a steadfast spirit within me.
¹¹Do not cast me from your presence
   or take your Holy Spirit from me.
¹²Restore to me the joy of your salvation
   and grant me a willing spirit, to sustain me.

¹³Then I will teach transgressors your ways,
   and sinners will turn back to you.
¹⁴Save me from bloodguilt, O God,
   the God who saves me,
   and my tongue will sing of your righteousness.
¹⁵O Lord, open my lips,
   and my mouth will declare your praise.
¹⁶You do not delight in sacrifice, or I would bring
     it;
   you do not take pleasure in burnt offerings.
¹⁷The sacrifices of God are[c] a broken spirit;
   a broken and contrite heart,
   O God, you will not despise.
¹⁸In your good pleasure make Zion prosper;
   build up the walls of Jerusalem.

[a] 6 The meaning of the Hebrew for this phrase is uncertain.
[b] 6 Or *you desired . . . ; / you taught*
[c] 17 Or *My sacrifice, O God, is*

¹⁹Then there will be righteous sacrifices,
    whole burnt offerings to delight you;
    then bulls will be offered on your altar.

Psalm 52

For the director of music. A *maskil*[a] of David. When Doeg the
Edomite had gone to Saul and told him: "David has gone to the
house of Ahimelech."

¹Why do you boast of evil, you mighty man?
    Why do you boast all day long,
    you who are a disgrace in the eyes of God?
²Your tongue plots destruction;
    it is like a sharpened razor,
    you who practice deceit.
³You love evil rather than good,
    falsehood rather than speaking the truth.   *Selah*
⁴You love every harmful word,
    O you deceitful tongue!

⁵Surely God will bring you down to everlasting
        ruin:
    He will snatch you up and tear you from your
        tent;
    he will uproot you from the land of the living.
                                        Selah

⁶The righteous will see and fear;
    they will laugh at him, saying,
⁷"Here now is the man
    who did not make God his stronghold
  but trusted in his great wealth
    and grew strong by destroying others!"

⁸But I am like an olive tree
    flourishing in the house of God;
I trust in God's unfailing love
    for ever and ever.
⁹I will praise you forever for what you have done;
    in your name I will hope, for your name is
        good.
    I will praise you in the presence of your saints.

aTitle: Probably a literary or musical term

Psalm 53

For the director of music. According to *mahalath*.[a] A *maskil*[b] of
David.

[1]The fool says in his heart,
    "There is no God."
They are corrupt, and their ways are vile;
    there is no one who does good.

[2]God looks down from heaven
    on the sons of men
to see if there are any who understand,
    any who seek God.
[3]Everyone has turned away,
    they have together become corrupt;
there is no one who does good,
    not even one.

[4]Will the evildoers never learn—
    those who devour my people as men eat bread
    and who do not call on God?
[5]There they were, overwhelmed with dread,
    where there was nothing to dread.
God scattered the bones of those who attacked
        you;
    you put them to shame, for God despised them.

[6]Oh, that salvation for Israel would come out of
        Zion!
    When God restores the fortunes of his people,
    let Jacob rejoice and Israel be glad!

Psalm 54

For the director of music. With stringed instruments. A *maskil*[b] of
David. When the Ziphites had gone to Saul and said, "Is not
David hiding among us?"

[1]Save me, O God, by your name;
    vindicate me by your might.

[a] Title: Probably a musical term
[b] Title: Probably a literary or musical term

²Hear my prayer, O God;
  listen to the words of my mouth.

³Strangers are attacking me;
  ruthless men seek my life—
  men without regard for God.   *Selah*

⁴Surely God is my help;
  the Lord is the one who sustains me.

⁵Let evil recoil on those who slander me;
  in your faithfulness destroy them.

⁶I will sacrifice a freewill offering to you;
  I will praise your name, O LORD,
  for it is good.
⁷For he has delivered me from all my troubles,
  and my eyes have looked in triumph on my
    foes.

Psalm 55

For the director of music. With stringed instruments. A *maskil*[a] of
David.

¹Listen to my prayer, O God,
  do not ignore my plea;
²   hear me and answer me.
My thoughts trouble me and I am distraught
³   at the voice of the enemy,
  at the stares of the wicked;
for they bring down suffering upon me
  and revile me in their anger.

⁴My heart is in anguish within me;
  the terrors of death assail me.
⁵Fear and trembling have beset me;
  horror has overwhelmed me.
⁶I said, "Oh, that I had the wings of a dove!
  I would fly away and be at rest—
⁷I would flee far away
  and stay in the desert;   *Selah*
⁸I would hurry to my place of shelter,
  far from the tempest and storm."

a Title: Probably a literary or musical term

⁹Confuse the wicked, O Lord, confound their
　　speech,
　for I see violence and strife in the city.
¹⁰Day and night they prowl about on its walls;
　　malice and abuse are within it.
¹¹Destructive forces are at work in the city;
　　threats and lies never leave its streets.

¹²If an enemy were insulting me,
　　I could endure it;
　if a foe were raising himself against me,
　　I could hide from him.
¹³But it is you, a man like myself,
　　my companion, my close friend,
¹⁴with whom I once enjoyed sweet fellowship
　　as we walked with the throng at the house of
　　　God.

¹⁵Let death take my enemies by surprise;
　　let them go down alive to the grave,ᵃ
　　for evil finds lodging among them.

¹⁶But I call to God,
　　and the LORD saves me.
¹⁷Evening, morning and noon
　　I cry out in distress,
　　and he hears my voice.
¹⁸He ransoms me unharmed
　　from the battle waged against me,
　　even though many oppose me.
¹⁹God, who is enthroned forever,
　　will hear them and afflict them—   *Selah*
　men who never change their ways
　　and have no fear of God.

²⁰My companion attacks his friends;
　　he violates his covenant.
²¹His speech is smooth as butter,
　　yet war is in his heart;
　his words are more soothing than oil,
　　yet they are drawn swords.

ᵃ15 Hebrew *Sheol*

²²Cast your cares on the LORD
    and he will sustain you;
    he will never let the righteous fall.
²³But you, O God, will bring down the wicked
    into the pit of corruption;
bloodthirsty and deceitful men
    will not live out half their days.

But as for me, I trust in you.

Psalm 56

For the director of music. To the tune of "A Dove on Distant Oaks." Of David. A *miktam.*[a] When the Philistines had seized him in Gath.

¹Be merciful to me, O God, for men hotly pursue
    me;
    all day long they press their attack.
²My slanderers pursue me all day long;
    many are attacking me in their pride.

³When I am afraid,
    I will trust in you.
⁴In God, whose word I praise,
    in God I trust; I will not be afraid.
    What can mortal man do to me?

⁵All day long they twist my words;
    they are always plotting to harm me.
⁶They conspire, they lurk,
    they watch my steps,
    eager to take my life.

⁷On no account let them escape;
    in your anger, O God, bring down the nations.
⁸Record my lament;
    list my tears on your scroll[b] —
    are they not in your record?

⁹Then my enemies will turn back
    when I call for help.
    By this I will know that God is for me.

[a] Title: Probably a literary or musical term
[b] 8 Or / *put my tears in your wineskin*

[10]In God, whose word I praise,
  in the LORD, whose word I praise—
[11]in God I trust; I will not be afraid.
  What can man do to me?

[12]I am under vows to you, O God;
  I will present my thank offerings to you.
[13]For you have delivered my soul from death
  and my feet from stumbling,
that I may walk before God
  in the light of life.[a]

Psalm 57

For the director of music. ⌊To the tune of⌋ "Do Not Destroy." Of
David. A *miktam*.[b] When he had fled from Saul into the cave.

[1]Have mercy on me, O God, have mercy on me,
  for in you my soul takes refuge.
I will take refuge in the shadow of your wings
  until the disaster has passed.

[2]I cry out to God Most High,
  to God, who fulfills ⌊his purpose⌋ for me.
[3]He sends from heaven and saves me,
  rebuking those who hotly pursue me;   *Selah*
God sends his love and his faithfulness.

[4]I am in the midst of lions;
  I lie among ravenous beasts—
men whose teeth are spears and arrows,
  whose tongues are sharp swords.

[5]Be exalted, O God, above the heavens;
  let your glory be over all the earth.

[6]They spread a net for my feet—
  I was bowed down in distress.
They dug a pit in my path—
  but they have fallen into it themselves.   *Selah*

[7]My heart is steadfast, O God,
  my heart is steadfast;

[a]13 Or *the land of the living*
[b]Title: Probably a literary or musical term

I will sing and make music.
8Awake, my soul!
   Awake, harp and lyre!
   I will awaken the dawn.

9I will praise you, O Lord, among the nations;
   I will sing of you among the peoples.
10For great is your love, reaching to the heavens;
   your faithfulness reaches to the skies.

11Be exalted, O God, above the heavens;
   let your glory be over all the earth.

Psalm 58

For the director of music. To the tune of, "Do Not Destroy." Of David. A *miktam.*[a]

1Do you rulers indeed speak justly?
   Do you judge uprightly among men?
2No, in your heart you devise injustice,
   and your hands mete out violence on the earth.
3Even from birth the wicked go astray;
   from the womb they are wayward and speak
     lies.
4Their venom is like the venom of a snake,
   like that of a cobra that has stopped its ears,
5that will not heed the tune of the charmer,
   however skillful the enchanter may be.

6Break the teeth in their mouths, O God;
   tear out, O Lord, the fangs of the lions!
7Let them vanish like water that flows away;
   when they draw the bow, let their arrows be
     blunted.
8Like a slug melting away as it moves along,
   like a stillborn child, may they not see the sun.

9Before your pots can feel the heat of the thorns—
   whether they be green or dry—the wicked will
     be swept away.[b]

a Title: Probably a literary or musical term
b 9 The meaning of the Hebrew for this verse is uncertain.

¹⁰The righteous will be glad when they are
                avenged,
        when they bathe their feet in the blood of the
            wicked.
¹¹Then men will say,
        "Surely the righteous still are rewarded;
        surely there is a God who judges the earth."

Psalm 59

For the director of music. To the tune of, "Do Not Destroy." Of
David. A *miktam*.[a] When Saul had sent men to watch David's
house in order to kill him.

¹Deliver me from my enemies, O God;
        protect me from those who rise up against me.
²Deliver me from evildoers
        and save me from bloodthirsty men.

³See how they lie in wait for me!
        Fierce men conspire against me
        for no offense or sin of mine, O LORD.
⁴I have done no wrong, yet they are ready to
                attack me.
        Arise to help me; look on my plight!
⁵O LORD God Almighty, the God of Israel,
        rouse yourself to punish all the nations;
        show no mercy to wicked traitors.   *Selah*

⁶They return at evening,
        snarling like dogs,
        and prowl about the city.
⁷See what they spew from their mouths—
        they spew out swords from their lips,
        and they say, "Who can hear us?"
⁸But you, O LORD, laugh at them;
        you scoff at all those nations.

⁹O my Strength, I watch for you;
        you, O God, are my fortress, ¹⁰my loving God.

        God will go before me

---

[a] Title: Probably a literary or musical term

and will let me gloat over those who slander
me.
[11]But do not kill them, O Lord our shield,[a]
or my people will forget.
In your might make them wander about,
and bring them down.
[12]For the sins of their mouths,
for the words of their lips,
let them be caught in their pride.
For the curses and lies they utter,
[13]   consume them in wrath,
consume them till they are no more.
Then it will be known to the ends of the earth
that God rules over Jacob. *Selah*

[14]They return at evening,
snarling like dogs,
and prowl about the city.
[15]They wander about for food
and howl if not satisfied.
[16]But I will sing of your strength,
in the morning I will sing of your love;
for you are my fortress,
my refuge in times of trouble.

[17]O my Strength, I sing praise to you;
you, O God, are my fortress, my loving God.

Psalm 60

For the director of music. To the tune of "The Lily of the
Covenant." A *miktam*[b] of David. For teaching. When he fought
Aram Naharaim[c] and Aram Zobah,[d] and when Joab returned and
struck down twelve thousand Edomites in the Valley of Salt.

[1]You have rejected us, O God, and burst forth
upon us;
you have been angry—now restore us!
[2]You have shaken the land and torn it open;
mend its fractures, for it is quaking.
[3]You have shown your people desperate times;

---

[a]11 Or *sovereign*   [b]Title: Probably a literary or musical term
[c]Title: That is, Arameans of Northwest Mesopotamia
[d]Title: That is, Arameans of central Syria

you have given us wine that makes us stagger.

⁴But for those who fear you, you have raised a
     banner
  to be unfurled against the bow.   *Selah*
⁵Save us and help us with your right hand,
  that those you love may be delivered.

⁶God has spoken from his sanctuary:
     "In triumph I will parcel out Shechem
     and measure off the Valley of Succoth.
⁷Gilead is mine, and Manasseh is mine;
     Ephraim is my helmet, Judah my scepter.
⁸Moab is my washbasin,
     upon Edom I toss my sandal;
     over Philistia I shout in triumph."

⁹Who will bring me to the fortified city?
  Who will lead me to Edom?
¹⁰Is it not you, O God, you who have rejected us
  and no longer go out with our armies?
¹¹Give us aid against the enemy,
  for the help of man is worthless.
¹²With God we will gain the victory,
  and he will trample down our enemies.

Psalm 61

For the director of music. With stringed instruments. Of David.

¹Hear my cry, O God;
  listen to my prayer.
²From the ends of the earth I call to you,
  I call as my heart grows faint;
  lead me to the rock that is higher than I.

³For you have been my refuge,
  a strong tower against the foe.
⁴I long to dwell in your tent forever
  and take refuge in the shelter of your wings.
                                             Selah
⁵For you have heard my vows, O God;
  you have given me the heritage of those who
       fear your name.

⁶Increase the days of the king's life,
   his years for many generations.
⁷May he be enthroned in God's presence forever;
   appoint your love and faithfulness to protect
     him.

⁸Then will I ever sing praise to your name
   and fulfill my vows day after day.

Psalm 62

For the director of music. To Jeduthun. A psalm of David.

¹My soul finds rest in God alone;
   my salvation comes from him.
²He alone is my rock and my salvation;
   he is my fortress, I will never be shaken.

³How long will you assault a man?
   Would all of you throw him down—
   this leaning wall, this tottering fence?
⁴They fully intend to topple him
   from his lofty place;
   they take delight in lies.
With their mouths they bless,
   but in their hearts they curse.   *Selah*

⁵Find rest, O my soul, in God alone;
   my hope comes from him.
⁶He alone is my rock and my salvation;
   he is my fortress, I will not be shaken.
⁷My salvation and my honor depend on God[a];
   he is my mighty rock, my refuge.
⁸Trust in him at all times, O people;
   pour out your hearts to him,
   for God is our refuge.   *Selah*

⁹Lowborn men are but a breath,
   the highborn are but a lie;
if weighed on a balance, they are nothing;
   together they are only a breath.
¹⁰Do not trust in extortion
   or take pride in stolen goods;

[a]7 Or / *God Most High is my salvation and my honor*

though your riches increase,
   do not set your heart on them.

[11]One thing God has spoken,
   two things have I heard:
that you, O God, are strong,
[12] and that you, O Lord, are loving.
Surely you will reward each person
   according to what he has done.

Psalm 63

A psalm of David. When he was in the desert of Judah.

[1]O God, you are my God,
   earnestly I seek you;
my soul thirsts for you,
   my body longs for you,
in a dry and weary land
   where there is no water.

[2]I have seen you in the sanctuary
   and beheld your power and your glory.
[3]Because your love is better than life,
   my lips will glorify you.
[4]I will praise you as long as I live,
   and in your name I will lift up my hands.
[5]My soul will be satisfied as with the richest of
     foods;
   with singing lips my mouth will praise you.

[6]On my bed I remember you;
   I think of you through the watches of the night.
[7]Because you are my help,
   I sing in the shadow of your wings.
[8]I stay close to you;
   your right hand upholds me.

[9]They who seek my life will be destroyed;
   they will go down to the depths of the earth.
[10]They will be given over to the sword
   and become food for jackals.

¹¹But the king will rejoice in God;
  all who swear by God's name will praise him,
  while the mouths of liars will be silenced.

Psalm 64

For the director of music. A psalm of David.

¹Hear me, O God, as I voice my complaint;
  protect my life from the threat of the enemy.

²Hide me from the conspiracy of the wicked,
  from that noisy crowd of evildoers,
³who sharpen their tongues like swords
  and aim their words like deadly arrows.
⁴They shoot from ambush at the innocent man;
  they shoot at him suddenly, without fear.

⁵They encourage each other in evil plans,
  they talk about hiding their snares;
  they say, "Who will see them*a*?"
⁶They plot injustice and say,
  "We have devised a perfect plan!"
  Surely the mind and heart of man are cunning.

⁷But God will shoot them with arrows;
  suddenly they will be struck down.
⁸He will turn their own tongues against them
  and bring them to ruin;
  all who see them will shake their heads in
    scorn.
⁹All mankind will fear;
  they will proclaim the works of God
  and ponder what he has done.

¹⁰Let the righteous rejoice in the LORD
  and take refuge in him;
  let all the upright in heart praise him!

---

a 5 Or *us*

Psalm 65

For the director of music. A psalm of David. A song.

[1]Praise awaits[a] you, O God, in Zion;
    to you our vows will be fulfilled.
[2]O you who hear prayer,
    to you all men will come.
[3]When we were overwhelmed by sins,
    you atoned for our transgressions.
[4]Blessed is the man you choose
    and bring near to live in your courts!
We are filled with the good things of your house,
    of your holy temple.

[5]You answer us with awesome deeds of
        righteousness,
    O God our Savior,
the hope of all the ends of the earth
    and of the farthest seas,
[6]who formed the mountains by your power,
    having armed yourself with strength,
[7]who stilled the roaring of the seas,
    the roaring of their waves,
    and the turmoil of the nations.
[8]Those living far away fear your wonders;
    where morning dawns and evening fades
    you call forth songs of joy.

[9]You care for the land and water it;
    you enrich it abundantly.
The streams of God are filled with water
    to provide the people with grain,
    for so you have ordained it.[b]
[10]You drench its furrows
    and level its ridges;
you soften it with showers
    and bless its crops.
[11]You crown the year with your bounty,
    and your carts overflow with abundance.

[a] 1 Or *befits;* the meaning of the Hebrew for this word is
uncertain.
[b] 9 Or *for that is how you prepare the land*

¹²The grasslands of the desert overflow;
  the hills are clothed with gladness.
¹³The meadows are covered with flocks
  and the valleys are mantled with grain;
  they shout for joy and sing.

Psalm 66

For the director of music. A song. A psalm.

¹Shout with joy to God, all the earth!
² Sing to the glory of his name;
  offer him glory and praise!
³Say to God, "How awesome are your deeds!
  So great is your power
  that your enemies cringe before you.
⁴All the earth bows down to you;
  they sing praise to you,
  they sing praise to your name."   *Selah*

⁵Come and see what God has done,
  how awesome his works in man's behalf!
⁶He turned the sea into dry land,
  they passed through the river on foot—
  come, let us rejoice in him.
⁷He rules forever by his power,
  his eyes watch the nations—
  let not the rebellious rise up against him. *Selah*

⁸Praise our God, O peoples,
  let the sound of his praise be heard;
⁹he has preserved our lives
  and kept our feet from slipping.
¹⁰For you, O God, tested us;
  you refined us like silver.
¹¹You brought us into prison
  and laid burdens on our backs.
¹²You let men ride over our heads;
  we went through fire and water,
  but you brought us to a place of abundance.

¹³I will come to your temple with burnt offerings
  and fulfill my vows to you—

[14]vows my lips promised and my mouth spoke
    when I was in trouble.
[15]I will sacrifice fat animals to you
    and an offering of rams;
    I will offer bulls and goats.   *Selah*

[16]Come and listen, all you who fear God;
    let me tell you what he has done for me.
[17]I cried out to him with my mouth;
    his praise was on my tongue.
[18]If I had cherished sin in my heart,
    the Lord would not have listened;
[19]but God has surely listened
    and heard my voice in prayer.
[20]Praise be to God,
    who has not rejected my prayer
    or withheld his love from me!

Psalm 67

For the director of music. With stringed instruments. A psalm. A
song.

[1]May God be gracious to us and bless us
    and make his face shine upon us;   *Selah*
[2]may your ways be known on earth,
    your salvation among all nations.

[3]May the peoples praise you, O God;
    may all the peoples praise you.
[4]May the nations be glad and sing for joy,
    for you rule the peoples justly
    and guide the nations of the earth.   *Selah*
[5]May the peoples praise you, O God;
    may all the peoples praise you.

[6]Then the land will yield its harvest,
    and God, our God, will bless us.
[7]God will bless us,
    and all the ends of the earth will fear him.

Psalm 68

For the director of music. Of David. A psalm. A song.

[1]May God arise, may his enemies be scattered;
  may his foes flee before him.
[2]As smoke is blown away by the wind,
  may you blow them away;
as wax melts before the fire,
  may the wicked perish before God.
[3]But may the righteous be glad
  and rejoice before God;
  may they be happy and joyful.

[4]Sing to God, sing praise to his name,
  extol him who rides on the clouds[a]—
his name is the LORD—
  and rejoice before him.
[5]A father to the fatherless, a defender of widows,
  is God in his holy dwelling.
[6]God sets the lonely in families,[b]
  he leads forth the prisoners with singing;
  but the rebellious live in a sun-scorched land.

[7]When you went out before your people, O God, ·
  when you marched through the wasteland, *Selah*
[8]the earth shook,
  the heavens poured down rain,
before God, the One of Sinai,
  before God, the God of Israel.
[9]You gave abundant showers, O God;
  you refreshed your weary inheritance.
[10]Your people settled in it,
  and from your bounty, O God, you provided for
    the poor.

[11]The Lord announced the word,
  and great was the company of those who
      proclaimed it:
[12]"Kings and armies flee in haste;
  in the camps men divide the plunder.
  [13]Even while you sleep among the campfires,[c]

a 4 Or / prepare the way for him who rides through the deserts
b 6 Or the desolate in a homeland   c 13 Or saddlebags

the wings of ˌmyˎ dove are sheathed with silver,
its feathers with shining gold."
[14]When the Almighty[a] scattered the kings in the
      land,
   it was like snow fallen on Zalmon.

[15]The mountains of Bashan are majestic mountains;
   rugged are the mountains of Bashan.
[16]Why gaze in envy, O rugged mountains,
   at the mountain where God chooses to reign,
   where the LORD himself will dwell forever?
[17]The chariots of God are tens of thousands
      and thousands of thousands;
   the Lord ˌhas comeˎ from Sinai into his
      sanctuary.
[18]When you ascended on high,
   you led captives in your train;
   you received gifts from men,
even from[b] the rebellious—
   that you,[c] O LORD God, might dwell there.

[19]Praise be to the Lord, to God our Savior,
   who daily bears our burdens.   Selah
[20]Our God is a God who saves;
   from the Sovereign LORD comes escape from
      death.

[21]Surely God will crush the heads of his enemies,
   the hairy crowns of those who go on in their
      sins.
[22]The Lord says, "I will bring you from Bashan;
   I will bring you from the depths of the sea,
[23]that you may plunge your feet in the blood of
      your foes,
   while the tongues of your dogs have their
      share."

[24]Your procession has come into view, O God,
   the procession of my God and King into the
      sanctuary.
[25]In front are the singers, after them the musicians;

a 14 Hebrew *Shaddai*   b 18 Or *gifts for men, / even*
c 18 Or *they*

> with them are the maidens playing
>> tambourines.
> 26Praise God in the great congregation;
>> praise the LORD in the assembly of Israel.
> 27There is the little tribe of Benjamin, leading them,
>> there the great throng of Judah's princes,
>> and there the princes of Zebulun and of
>>> Naphtali.

> 28Summon your power, O Goda;
>> show us your strength, O God, as you have
>>> done before.
> 29Because of your temple at Jerusalem
>> kings will bring you gifts.
> 30Rebuke the beast among the reeds,
>> the herd of bulls among the calves of the
>>> nations.
> Humbled, may it bring bars of silver.
> Scatter the nations who delight in war.
> 31Envoys will come from Egypt;
>> Cushb will submit herself to God.

> 32Sing to God, O kingdoms of the earth,
>> sing praise to the Lord,   *Selah*
> 33to him who rides the ancient skies above,
>> who thunders with mighty voice.
> 34Proclaim the power of God,
>> whose majesty is over Israel,
>> whose power is in the skies.
> 35You are awesome, O God, in your sanctuary;
>> the God of Israel gives power and strength to
>>> his people.

> Praise be to God!

Psalm 69

For the director of music. To the tune of, "Lilies." Of David.

> 1Save me, O God,
>> for the waters have come up to my neck.

a 28 Many Hebrew manuscripts, Septuagint and Syriac; most
Hebrew manuscripts *Your God has summoned power for you*
b 31 That is, the upper Nile region

²I sink in the miry depths,
   where there is no foothold.
I have come into the deep waters;
   the floods engulf me.
³I am worn out calling for help;
   my throat is parched.
My eyes fail,
   looking for my God.
⁴Those who hate me without reason
   outnumber the hairs of my head;
many are my enemies without cause,
   those who seek to destroy me.
I am forced to restore
   what I did not steal.

⁵You know my folly, O God;
   my guilt is not hidden from you.

⁶May those who hope in you
   not be disgraced because of me,
   O Lord, the LORD Almighty;
may those who seek you
   not be put to shame because of me,
   O God of Israel.
⁷For I endure scorn for your sake,
   and shame covers my face.
⁸I am a stranger to my brothers,
   an alien to my own mother's sons;
⁹for zeal for your house consumes me,
   and the insults of those who insult you fall
      on me.
¹⁰When I weep and fast,
   I must endure scorn;
¹¹when I put on sackcloth,
   people make sport of me.
¹²Those who sit at the gate mock me,
   and I am the song of the drunkards.

¹³But I pray to you, O LORD,
   in the time of your favor;
in your great love, O God,
   answer me with your sure salvation.
¹⁴Rescue me from the mire,

do not let me sink;
   deliver me from those who hate me,
     from the deep waters.
15Do not let the floodwaters engulf me
   or the depths swallow me up
   or the pit close its mouth over me.
16Answer me, O LORD, out of the goodness of your
     love;
   in your great mercy turn to me.
17Do not hide your face from your servant;
   answer me quickly, for I am in trouble.
18Come near and rescue me;
   redeem me because of my foes.

19You know how I am scorned, disgraced and
     shamed;
   all my enemies are before you.
20Scorn has broken my heart
   and has left me helpless;
 I looked for sympathy, but there was none,
   for comforters, but I found none.
21They put gall in my food
   and gave me vinegar for my thirst.

22May the table set before them become a snare;
   may it become retribution anda a trap.
23May their eyes be darkened so they cannot see,
   and their backs be bent forever.
24Pour out your wrath on them;
   let your fierce anger overtake them.
25May their place be deserted;
   let there be no one to dwell in their tents.
26For they persecute those you wound
   and talk about the pain of those you hurt.
27Charge them with crime upon crime;
   do not let them share in your salvation.
28May they be blotted out of the book of life
   and not be listed with the righteous.

29I am in pain and distress;
   may your salvation, O God, protect me.

a 22 Or *snare* / *and their fellowship become*

³⁰I will praise God's name in song
    and glorify him with thanksgiving.
³¹This will please the LORD more than an ox,
    more than a bull with its horns and hoofs.
³²The poor will see and be glad—
    you who seek God, may your hearts live!
³³The LORD hears the needy
    and does not despise his captive people.

³⁴Let heaven and earth praise him,
    the seas and all that move in them,
³⁵for God will save Zion
    and rebuild the cities of Judah.
Then people will settle there and possess it;
³⁶   the children of his servants will inherit it,
    and those who love his name will dwell there.

Psalm 70

For the director of music. Of David. A petition.

¹Hasten, O God, to save me;
    O LORD, come quickly to help me.
²May those who seek my life
    be put to shame and confusion;
may all who desire my ruin
    be turned back in disgrace.
³May those who say to me, "Aha! Aha!"
    turn back because of their shame.
⁴But may all who seek you
    rejoice and be glad in you;
may those who love your salvation always say,
    "Let God be exalted!"

⁵Yet I am poor and needy;
    come quickly to me, O God.
You are my help and my deliverer;
    O LORD, do not delay.

Psalm 71

¹In you, O LORD, I have taken refuge;
    let me never be put to shame.
²Rescue me and deliver me in your righteousness;

turn your ear to me and save me.
³Be my rock of refuge,
to which I can always go;
give the command to save me,
for you are my rock and my fortress.
⁴Deliver me, O my God, from the hand of the
wicked,
from the grasp of evil and cruel men.

⁵For you have been my hope, O Sovereign LORD,
my confidence since my youth.
⁶From birth I have relied on you;
you brought me forth from my mother's womb.
I will ever praise you.
⁷I have become like a portent to many,
but you are my strong refuge.
⁸My mouth is filled with your praise,
declaring your splendor all day long.

⁹Do not cast me away when I am old;
do not forsake me when my strength is gone.
¹⁰For my enemies speak against me;
those who wait to kill me conspire together.
¹¹They say, "God has forsaken him;
pursue him and seize him,
for no one will rescue him."
¹²Be not far from me, O God;
come quickly, O my God, to help me.
¹³May my accusers perish in shame;
may those who want to harm me
be covered with scorn and disgrace.

¹⁴But as for me, I will always have hope;
I will praise you more and more.
¹⁵My mouth will tell of your righteousness,
of your salvation all day long,
though I know not its measure.
¹⁶I will come and proclaim your mighty acts, O
Sovereign LORD;
I will proclaim your righteousness, yours alone.
¹⁷Since my youth, O God, you have taught me,
and to this day I declare your marvelous deeds.
¹⁸Even when I am old and gray,

    do not forsake me, O God,
till I declare your power to the next generation,
    your might to all who are to come.

[19]Your righteousness reaches to the skies, O God,
    you who have done great things.
    Who, O God, is like you?
[20]Though you have made me see troubles, many
        and bitter,
    you will restore my life again;
from the depths of the earth
    you will again bring me up.
[21]You will increase my honor
    and comfort me once again.

[22]I will praise you with the harp
    for your faithfulness, O my God;
I will sing praise to you with the lyre,
    O Holy One of Israel.
[23]My lips will shout for joy
    when I sing praise to you—
    I, whom you have redeemed.
[24]My tongue will tell of your righteous acts
    all day long,
for those who wanted to harm me
    have been put to shame and confusion.

Psalm 72

Of Solomon.

[1]Endow the king with your justice, O God,
    the royal son with your righteousness.

[2]He will[a] judge your people in righteousness,
    your afflicted ones with justice.
[3]The mountains will bring prosperity to the people,
    the hills the fruit of righteousness.
[4]He will defend the afflicted among the people
    and save the children of the needy;
    he will crush the oppressor.

---

a 2 Or *May he*; similarly in verses 3–11 and 17

⁵He will endure[a] as long as the sun,
  as long as the moon, through all generations.
⁶He will be like rain falling on a mown field,
  like showers watering the earth.
⁷In his days the righteous will flourish;
  prosperity will abound till the moon is no more.

⁸He will rule from sea to sea
  and from the River[b] to the ends of the earth.
⁹The desert tribes will bow before him
  and his enemies will lick the dust.
¹⁰The kings of Tarshish and of distant shores
  will bring tribute to him;
 the kings of Sheba and Seba
  will present him gifts.
¹¹All kings will bow down to him
  and all nations will serve him.

¹²For he will deliver the needy who cry out,
  the afflicted who have no one to help.
¹³He will take pity on the weak and the needy
  and save the needy from death.
¹⁴He will rescue them from oppression and
      violence,
  for precious is their blood in his sight.

¹⁵Long may he live!
  May gold from Sheba be given him.
 May people ever pray for him
  and bless him all day long.
¹⁶Let grain abound throughout the land;
  on the tops of the hills may it sway.
 Let its fruit flourish like Lebanon;
  let it thrive like the grass of the field.
¹⁷May his name endure forever;
  may it continue as long as the sun.

 All nations will be blessed through him,
  and they will call him blessed.

¹⁸Praise be to the LORD God, the God of Israel,

[a]5 Septuagint; Hebrew / *You will be feared*
[b]8 That is, the Euphrates

who alone does marvelous deeds.
¹⁹Praise be to his glorious name forever;
   may the whole earth be filled with his glory.
          Amen and Amen.

²⁰This concludes the prayers of David son of Jesse.

BOOK III

Psalms 73-89

Psalm 73

A psalm of Asaph.

¹Surely God is good to Israel,
   to those who are pure in heart.

²But as for me, my feet had almost slipped;
   I had nearly lost my foothold.
³For I envied the arrogant
   when I saw the prosperity of the wicked.

⁴They have no struggles;
   their bodies are healthy and strong.[a]
⁵They are free from the burdens common to man;
   they are not plagued by human ills.
⁶Therefore pride is their necklace;
   they clothe themselves with violence.
⁷From their callous hearts comes iniquity[b];
   the evil conceits of their minds know no limits.
⁸They scoff, and speak with malice;
   in their arrogance they threaten oppression.
⁹Their mouths lay claim to heaven,
   and their tongues take possession of the earth.
¹⁰Therefore their people turn to them
   and drink up waters in abundance.[c]
¹¹They say, "How can God know?
   Does the Most High have knowledge?"

---

a 4 With a different word division of the Hebrew; Masoretic Text
struggles at their death; / their bodies are healthy
b 7 Syriac (see also Septuagint); Hebrew *Their eyes bulge with fat*
c 10 The meaning of the Hebrew for this verse is uncertain.

¹²This is what the wicked are like—
    always carefree, they increase in wealth.

¹³Surely in vain have I kept my heart pure;
    in vain have I washed my hands in innocence.
¹⁴All day long I have been plagued;
    I have been punished every morning.

¹⁵If I had said, "I will speak thus,"
    I would have betrayed this generation of your
        children.
¹⁶When I tried to understand all this,
    it was oppressive to me
¹⁷till I entered the sanctuary of God;
    then I understood their final destiny.

¹⁸Surely you place them on slippery ground;
    you cast them down to ruin.
¹⁹How suddenly are they destroyed,
    completely swept away by terrors!
²⁰As a dream when one awakes,
    so when you arise, O Lord,
    you will despise them as fantasies.

²¹When my heart was grieved
    and my spirit embittered,
²²I was senseless and ignorant;
    I was a brute beast before you.

²³Yet I am always with you;
    you hold me by my right hand.
²⁴You guide me with your counsel,
    and afterward you will take me into glory.
²⁵Whom have I in heaven but you?
    And being with you, I desire nothing on earth.
²⁶My flesh and my heart may fail,
    but God is the strength of my heart
    and my portion forever.

²⁷Those who are far from you will perish;
    you destroy all who are unfaithful to you.
²⁸But as for me, it is good to be near God.
    I have made the Sovereign LORD my refuge;
    I will tell of all your deeds.

Psalm 74

A *maskil*[a] of Asaph.

¹Why have you rejected us forever, O God?
  Why does your anger smolder against the sheep
    of your pasture?
²Remember the people you purchased of old,
  the tribe you redeemed as your inheritance—
  Mount Zion, where you dwelt.

³Pick your way through these everlasting ruins,
  all this destruction the enemy has brought on
    the sanctuary.
⁴Your foes roared in the place where you met
    with us;
  they set up their standards as signs.
⁵They behaved like men wielding axes
  to cut through a thicket of trees.
⁶They smashed all the carved paneling
  with their axes and hatchets.
⁷They burned your sanctuary to the ground;
  they defiled the dwelling place of your Name.
⁸They said in their hearts, "We will crush them
    completely!"
  They burned every place where God was
    worshiped in the land.

⁹We are given no miraculous signs;
  no prophets are left,
  and none of us knows how long this will be.
¹⁰How long will the enemy mock you, O God?
  Will the foe revile your name forever?
¹¹Why do you hold back your hand, your right
    hand?
  Take it from the folds of your garment and
    destroy them!

¹²But you, O God, are my king from of old;
  you bring salvation upon the earth.
¹³It was you who split open the sea by your power;

---

a Title: Probably a literary or musical term

you broke the heads of the monster in the
waters.
¹⁴It was you who crushed the heads of Leviathan
and gave him as food to the creatures of the
desert.
¹⁵It was you who opened up springs and streams;
you dried up the ever flowing rivers.
¹⁶The day is yours, and yours also the night;
you established the sun and moon.
¹⁷It was you who set all the boundaries of the earth;
you made both summer and winter.

¹⁸Remember how the enemy has mocked you, O
LORD,
how foolish people have reviled your name.
¹⁹Do not hand over the life of your dove to wild
beasts;
do not forget the lives of your afflicted people
forever.
²⁰Have regard for your covenant,
because haunts of violence fill the dark places of
the land.
²¹Do not let the oppressed retreat in disgrace;
may the poor and needy praise your name.

²²Rise up, O God, and defend your cause;
remember how fools mock you all day long.
²³Do not ignore the clamor of your adversaries,
the uproar of your enemies, which rises
continually.

Psalm 75

For the director of music. To the tune of, "Do Not Destroy." A
psalm of Asaph. A song.

¹We give thanks to you, O God,
we give thanks, for your Name is near;
men tell of your wonderful deeds.

²You say, "I choose the appointed time;
it is I who judge uprightly.
³When the earth and all its people quake,
it is I who hold its pillars firm.   *Selah*

⁴To the arrogant I say, 'Boast no more,'
    and to the wicked, 'Do not lift up your horns.
⁵Do not lift your horns against heaven;
    do not speak with outstretched neck.' ''

⁶No one from the east or the west
    or from the desert can exalt a man.
⁷But it is God who judges:
    He brings one down, he exalts another.
⁸In the hand of the LORD is a cup
    full of foaming wine mixed with spices;
  he pours it out, and all the wicked of the earth
    drink it down to its very dregs.

⁹As for me, I will declare this forever;
    I will sing praise to the God of Jacob.
¹⁰I will cut off the horns of all the wicked,
    but the horns of the righteous will be lifted up.

Psalm 76

For the director of music. With stringed instruments. A psalm of
Asaph. A song.

¹In Judah God is known;
    his name is great in Israel.
²His tent is in Salem,
    his dwelling place in Zion.
³There he broke the flashing arrows,
    the shields and the swords, the weapons of war.
                                                                Selah

⁴You are resplendent with light,
    more majestic than mountains rich with game.
⁵Valiant men lie plundered,
    they sleep their last sleep;
  not one of the warriors
    can lift his hands.
⁶At your rebuke, O God of Jacob,
    both horse and chariot lie still.
⁷You alone are to be feared.
    Who can stand before you when you are angry?
⁸From heaven you pronounced judgment,
    and the land feared and was quiet—

⁹when you, O God, rose up to judge,
    to save all the afflicted of the land. *Selah*
¹⁰Surely your wrath against men brings you praise,
    and the survivors of your wrath are restrained.[a]

¹¹Make vows to the LORD your God and fulfill them;
    let all the neighboring lands
    bring gifts to the One to be feared.
¹²He breaks the spirit of rulers;
    he is feared by the kings of the earth.

Psalm 77

For the director of music. To Jeduthun. Of Asaph. A psalm.

¹I cried out to God for help;
    I cried out to God to hear me.
²When I was in distress, I sought the Lord;
    at night I stretched out untiring hands
    and my soul refused to be comforted.

³I remembered you, O God, and I groaned;
    I mused, and my spirit grew faint. *Selah*
⁴You kept my eyes from closing;
    I was too troubled to speak.
⁵I thought about the former days,
    the years of long ago;
⁶I remembered my songs in the night.
    My heart mused and my spirit inquired:

⁷"Will the Lord reject us forever?
    Will he never show his favor again?
⁸Has his unfailing love vanished forever?
    Has his promise failed for all time?
⁹Has God forgotten to be merciful?
    Has he in anger withheld his compassion?"

Selah

¹⁰Then I thought, "To this I will appeal:
    the years of the right hand of the Most High."
¹¹I will remember the deeds of the LORD;
    yes, I will remember your miracles of long ago.

a 10 Or *Surely the wrath of men brings you praise, / and with the
remainder of wrath you arm yourself*

¹²I will meditate on all your works
    and consider all your mighty deeds.

¹³Your ways, O God, are holy.
    What god is so great as our God?
¹⁴You are the God who performs miracles;
    you display your power among the peoples.
¹⁵With your mighty arm you redeemed your people,
    the descendants of Jacob and Joseph.   *Selah*

¹⁶The waters saw you, O God,
    the waters saw you and writhed;
    the very depths were convulsed.
¹⁷The clouds poured down water,
    the skies resounded with thunder;
    your arrows flashed back and forth.
¹⁸Your thunder was heard in the whirlwind,
    your lightning lit up the world;
    the earth trembled and quaked.
¹⁹Your path led through the sea,
    your way through the mighty waters,
    though your footprints were not seen.

²⁰You led your people like a flock
    by the hand of Moses and Aaron.

Psalm 78

A *maskil*[a] of Asaph.

¹O my people, hear my teaching;
    listen to the words of my mouth.
²I will open my mouth in parables,
    I will utter things hidden from of old—
³things we have heard and known,
    things our fathers have told us.
⁴We will not hide them from their children;
    we will tell the next generation
the praiseworthy deeds of the LORD,
    his power, and the wonders he has done.
⁵He decreed statutes for Jacob
    and established the law in Israel,

---

[a] Title: Probably a literary or musical term

which he commanded our forefathers
    to teach their children,
⁶so the next generation would know them,
    even the children yet to be born,
    and they in turn would tell their children.
⁷Then they would put their trust in God
    and would not forget his deeds
    but would keep his commands.
⁸They would not be like their forefathers—
    a stubborn and rebellious generation,
    whose hearts were not loyal to God,
    whose spirits were not faithful to him.

⁹The men of Ephraim, though armed with bows,
    turned back on the day of battle;
¹⁰they did not keep God's covenant
    and refused to live by his law.
¹¹They forgot what he had done,
    the wonders he had shown them.
¹²He did miracles in the sight of their fathers
    in the land of Egypt, in the region of Zoan.
¹³He divided the sea and led them through;
    he made the water stand firm like a wall.
¹⁴He guided them with the cloud by day
    and with light from the fire all night.
¹⁵He split the rocks in the desert
    and gave them water as abundant as the seas;
¹⁶he brought streams out of a rocky crag
    and made water flow down like rivers.

¹⁷But they continued to sin against him,
    rebelling in the desert against the Most High.
¹⁸They willfully put God to the test
    by demanding the food they craved.
¹⁹They spoke against God, saying,
    "Can God spread a table in the desert?
²⁰When he struck the rock, water gushed out,
    and streams flowed abundantly.
But can he also give us food?
    Can he supply meat for his people?"
²¹When the LORD heard them, he was very angry;
    his fire broke out against Jacob,

and his wrath rose against Israel,
²²for they did not believe in God
    or trust in his deliverance.
²³Yet he gave a command to the skies above
    and opened the doors of the heavens;
²⁴he rained down manna for the people to eat,
    he gave them the grain of heaven.
²⁵Men ate the bread of angels;
    he sent them all the food they could eat.
²⁶He let loose the east wind from the heavens
    and led forth the south wind by his power.
²⁷He rained meat down on them like dust,
    flying birds like sand on the seashore.
²⁸He made them fall inside their camp,
    all around their tents.
²⁹They ate till they had more than enough,
    for he had given them what they craved.
³⁰But before they turned from the food they craved,
    even while it was still in their mouths,
³¹God's anger rose against them;
    he put to death the sturdiest among them,
    cutting down the young men of Israel.

³²In spite of all this, they kept on sinning;
    in spite of his wonders, they did not believe.
³³So he ended their days in futility
    and their years in terror.
³⁴Whenever God slew them, they would seek him;
    they eagerly turned to him again.
³⁵They remembered that God was their Rock,
    that God Most High was their Redeemer.
³⁶But then they would flatter him with their
        mouths,
    lying to him with their tongues;
³⁷their hearts were not loyal to him,
    they were not faithful to his covenant.
³⁸Yet he was merciful;
    he atoned for their iniquities
    and did not destroy them.
Time after time he restrained his anger
    and did not stir up his full wrath.

³⁹He remembered that they were but flesh,
  a passing breeze that does not return.

⁴⁰How often they rebelled against him in the desert
  and grieved him in the wasteland!
⁴¹Again and again they put God to the test;
  they vexed the Holy One of Israel.
⁴²They did not remember his power—
  the day he redeemed them from the oppressor,
⁴³the day he displayed his miraculous signs in
      Egypt,
  his wonders in the region of Zoan.
⁴⁴He turned their rivers to blood;
  they could not drink from their streams.
⁴⁵He sent swarms of flies that devoured them
  and frogs that devastated them.
⁴⁶He gave their crops to the grasshopper,
  their produce to the locust.
⁴⁷He destroyed their vines with hail
  and their sycamore-figs with sleet.
⁴⁸He gave over their cattle to the hail,
  their livestock to bolts of lightning.
⁴⁹He unleashed against them his hot anger,
  his wrath, indignation and hostility—
  a band of destroying angels.
⁵⁰He prepared a path for his anger;
  he did not spare them from death
  but gave them over to the plague.
⁵¹He struck down all the firstborn of Egypt,
  the firstfruits of manhood in the tents of Ham.
⁵²But he brought his people out like a flock;
  he led them like sheep through the desert.
⁵³He guided them safely, so they were unafraid;
  but the sea engulfed their enemies.
⁵⁴Thus he brought them to the border of his holy
      land,
  to the hill country his right hand had taken.
⁵⁵He drove out nations before them
  and allotted their lands to them as an
      inheritance;
  he settled the tribes of Israel in their homes.

⁵⁶But they put God to the test
    and rebelled against the Most High;
    they did not keep his statutes.
⁵⁷Like their fathers they were disloyal and faithless,
    as unreliable as a faulty bow.
⁵⁸They angered him with their high places;
    they aroused his jealousy with their idols.
⁵⁹When God heard them, he was very angry;
    he rejected Israel completely.
⁶⁰He abandoned the tabernacle of Shiloh,
    the tent he had set up among men.
⁶¹He sent the ark of his might into captivity,
    his splendor into the hands of the enemy.
⁶²He gave his people over to the sword;
    he was very angry with his inheritance.
⁶³Fire consumed their young men,
    and their maidens had no wedding songs;
⁶⁴their priests were put to the sword,
    and their widows could not weep.

⁶⁵Then the Lord awoke as from sleep,
    as a man wakes from the stupor of wine.
⁶⁶He beat back his enemies;
    he put them to everlasting shame.
⁶⁷Then he rejected the tents of Joseph,
    he did not choose the tribe of Ephraim;
⁶⁸but he chose the tribe of Judah,
    Mount Zion, which he loved.
⁶⁹He built his sanctuary like the high mountains,
    like the earth that he established forever.
⁷⁰He chose David his servant
    and took him from the sheep pens;
⁷¹from tending the sheep he brought him
    to be the shepherd of his people Jacob,
    of Israel his inheritance.
⁷²And David shepherded them with integrity of
        heart;
    with skillful hands he led them.

Psalm 79

A psalm of Asaph.

¹O God, the nations have invaded your
       inheritance;
  they have defiled your holy temple,
  they have reduced Jerusalem to rubble.
²They have given the dead bodies of your servants
  as food to the birds of the air,
    the flesh of your saints to the beasts of the
       earth.
³They have poured out blood like water
  all around Jerusalem,
  and there is no one to bury the dead.
⁴We are objects of reproach to our neighbors,
  of scorn and derision to those around us.

⁵How long, O LORD? Will you be angry forever?
  How long will your jealousy burn like fire?
⁶Pour out your wrath on the nations
  that do not acknowledge you,
 on the kingdoms
  that do not call on your name;
⁷for they have devoured Jacob
  and destroyed his homeland.
⁸Do not hold against us the sins of the fathers;
  may your mercy come quickly to meet us,
  for we are in desperate need.

⁹Help us, O God our Savior,
  for the glory of your name;
 deliver us and atone for our sins
  for your name's sake.
¹⁰Why should the nations say,
  "Where is their God?"
 Before our eyes, make known among the nations
  that you avenge the outpoured blood of your
      servants.
¹¹May the groans of the prisoners come before you;
  by the strength of your arm
  preserve those condemned to die.

¹²Pay back into the laps of our neighbors seven
        times
    the reproach they have hurled at you, O Lord.
¹³Then we your people, the sheep of your pasture,
    will praise you forever;
from generation to generation
    we will recount your praise.

Psalm 80

For the director of music. To the tune of "The Lilies of the
Covenant." Of Asaph. A psalm.

¹Hear us, O Shepherd of Israel,
    you who lead Joseph like a flock;
you who sit enthroned between the cherubim,
        shine forth
² before Ephraim, Benjamin and Manasseh.
Awaken your might;
    come and save us.

³Restore us, O God;
    make your face shine upon us,
    that we may be saved.

⁴O LORD God Almighty,
    how long will your anger smolder
against the prayers of your people?
⁵You have fed them with the bread of tears;
    you have made them drink tears by the bowlful.
⁶You have made us a source of contention to our
        neighbors,
    and our enemies mock us.

⁷Restore us, O God Almighty;
    make your face shine upon us,
    that we may be saved.

⁸You brought a vine out of Egypt;
    you drove out the nations and planted it.
⁹You cleared the ground for it,
    and it took root and filled the land.
¹⁰The mountains were covered with its shade,
    the mighty cedars with its branches.

11It sent out its boughs to the Sea,[a]
  its shoots as far as the River.[b]

12Why have you broken down its walls
  so that all who pass by pick its grapes?
13Boars from the forest ravage it
  and the creatures of the field feed on it.
14Return to us, O God Almighty!
  Look down from heaven and see!
 Watch over this vine,
15 the root your right hand has planted,
  the son[c] you have raised up for yourself.

16Your vine is cut down, it is burned with fire;
  at your rebuke your people perish.
17Let your hand rest on the man at your right hand,
  the son of man you have raised up for yourself.
18Then we will not turn away from you;
  revive us, and we will call on your name.

19Restore us, O LORD God Almighty;
  make your face shine upon us,
  that we may be saved.

Psalm 81

For the director of music. According to *gittith*.[d] Of Asaph.

1Sing for joy to God our strength;
  shout aloud to the God of Jacob!
2Begin the music, strike the tambourine,
  play the melodious harp and lyre.

3Sound the ram's horn at the New Moon,
  and when the moon is full, on the day of our
        Feast;
4this is a decree for Israel,
  an ordinance of the God of Jacob.
5He established it as a statute for Joseph
  when he went out against Egypt,

a *11* Probably the Mediterranean   b *11* That is, the Euphrates
c *15* Or *branch*   d Title: Probably a musical term

where we heard a language we did not
   understand.[a]

[6]He says, "I removed the burden from their
      shoulders;
   their hands were set free from the basket.
[7]In your distress you called and I rescued you,
   I answered you out of a thundercloud;
   I tested you at the waters of Meribah.   *Selah*

[8]"Hear, O my people, and I will warn you—
   if you would but listen to me, O Israel!
[9]You shall have no foreign god among you;
   you shall not bow down to an alien god.
[10]I am the LORD your God,
   who brought you up out of Egypt.
   Open wide your mouth and I will fill it.

[11]"But my people would not listen to me;
   Israel would not submit to me.
[12]So I gave them over to their stubborn hearts
   to follow their own devices.

[13]"If my people would but listen to me,
   if Israel would follow my ways,
[14]how quickly would I subdue their enemies
   and turn my hand against their foes!
[15]Those who hate the LORD would cringe before
      him,
   and their punishment would last forever.
[16]But you would be fed with the finest of wheat;
   with honey from the rock I would satisfy you."

Psalm 82

A psalm of Asaph.

[1]God presides in the great assembly;
   he gives judgment among the "gods":

[2]"How long will you[b] defend the unjust
   and show partiality to the wicked?   *Selah*
[3]Defend the cause of the weak and fatherless;

[a]5 Or / *and we heard a voice we had not known*
[b]2 The Hebrew is plural.

maintain the rights of the poor and oppressed.
⁴Rescue the weak and needy;
    deliver them from the hand of the wicked.

⁵"They know nothing, they understand nothing.
    They walk about in darkness;
    all the foundations of the earth are shaken.

⁶"I said, 'You are "gods";
    you are all sons of the Most High.'
⁷But you will die like mere men;
    you will fall like every other ruler."

⁸Rise up, O God, judge the earth,
    for all the nations are your inheritance.

Psalm 83

A song. A psalm of Asaph.

¹O God, do not keep silent;
    be not quiet, O God, be not still.
²See how your enemies are astir,
    how your foes rear their heads.
³With cunning they conspire against your people;
    they plot against those you cherish.
⁴"Come," they say, "let us destroy them as a
        nation,
    that the name of Israel be remembered no
        more."

⁵With one mind they plot together;
    they form an alliance against you—
⁶the tents of Edom and the Ishmaelites,
    of Moab and the descendants of Hagar,
⁷Gebal,ᵃ Ammon and Amalek,
    Philistia, with the people of Tyre.
⁸Even Assyria has joined them
    to lend strength to the descendants of Lot. *Selah*

⁹Do to them as you did to Midian,
    as you did to Sisera and Jabin at the river
        Kishon,

ᵃ7 That is, Byblos

[10]who perished at Endor
   and became like refuse on the ground.
[11]Make their nobles like Oreb and Zeeb,
   all their princes like Zebah and Zalmunna,
[12]who said, "Let us take possession
   of the pasturelands of God."

[13]Make them like tumbleweed, O my God,
   like chaff before the wind.
[14]As fire consumes the forest
   or a flame sets the mountains ablaze,
[15]so pursue them with your tempest
   and terrify them with your storm.
[16]Cover their faces with shame
   so that men will seek your name, O LORD.

[17]May they ever be ashamed and dismayed;
   may they perish in disgrace.
[18]Let them know that you, whose name is the
   LORD—
   that you alone are the Most High over all the
   earth.

Psalm 84

For the director of music. According to *gittith*.[a] Of the Sons of
Korah. A psalm.

[1]How lovely is your dwelling place,
   O LORD Almighty!
[2]My soul yearns, even faints
   for the courts of the LORD;
my heart and my flesh cry out
   for the living God.

[3]Even the sparrow has found a home,
   and the swallow a nest for herself,
   where she may have her young—
a place near your altar,
   O LORD Almighty, my King and my God.
[4]Blessed are those who dwell in your house;
   they are ever praising you.   *Selah*

---

[a]Title: Probably a musical term

⁵Blessed are those whose strength is in you,
    who have set their hearts on pilgrimage.
⁶As they pass through the Valley of Baca,
    they make it a place of springs;
    the autumn rains also cover it with pools.ᵃ
⁷They go from strength to strength
    till each appears before God in Zion.

⁸Hear my prayer, O Lᴏʀᴅ God Almighty;
    listen to me, O God of Jacob.   *Selah*
⁹Look upon our shield,ᵇ O God;
    look with favor on your anointed one.

¹⁰Better is one day in your courts
    than a thousand elsewhere;
I would rather be a doorkeeper in the house of my
    God
    than dwell in the tents of the wicked.
¹¹For the Lᴏʀᴅ God is a sun and shield;
    the Lᴏʀᴅ bestows favor and honor;
no good thing does he withhold
    from those whose walk is blameless.

¹²O Lᴏʀᴅ Almighty,
    blessed is the man who trusts in you.

Psalm 85

For the director of music. Of the Sons of Korah. A psalm.

¹You showed favor to your land, O Lᴏʀᴅ;
    you restored the fortunes of Jacob.
²You forgave the iniquity of your people
    and covered all their sins.   *Selah*
³You set aside all your wrath
    and turned from your fierce anger.

⁴Restore us again, O God our Savior,
    and put away your displeasure toward us.
⁵Will you be angry with us forever?
    Will you prolong your anger through all
        generations?
⁶Will you not revive us again,

ᵃ 5 Or *blessings*   ᵇ 9 Or *sovereign*

that your people may rejoice in you?
⁷Show us your unfailing love, O LORD,
and grant us your salvation.

⁸I will listen to what God the LORD will say;
he promises peace to his people, his saints—
but let them not return to folly.
⁹Surely his salvation is near those who fear him,
that his glory may dwell in our land.

¹⁰Love and faithfulness meet together;
righteousness and peace kiss each other.
¹¹Faithfulness springs forth from the earth,
and righteousness looks down from heaven.
¹²The LORD will indeed give what is good,
and our land will yield its harvest.
¹³Righteousness goes before him
and prepares the way for his steps.

Psalm 86

A prayer of David.

¹Hear, O LORD, and answer me,
for I am poor and needy.
²Guard my life, for I am devoted to you.
You are my God; save your servant
who trusts in you.
³Have mercy on me, O Lord,
for I call to you all day long.
⁴Bring joy to your servant,
for to you, O Lord,
I lift up my soul.

⁵You are kind and forgiving, O Lord,
abounding in love to all who call to you.
⁶Hear my prayer, O LORD;
listen to my cry for mercy.
⁷In the day of my trouble I will call to you,
for you will answer me.

⁸Among the gods there is none like you, O Lord;
no deeds can compare with yours.
⁹All the nations you have made

will come and worship before you, O Lord;
    they will bring glory to your name.
[10]For you are great and do marvelous deeds;
    you alone are God.

[11]Teach me your way, O Lord,
    and I will walk in your truth;
  give me an undivided heart,
    that I may fear your name.
[12]I will praise you, O Lord my God, with all my
        heart;
    I will glorify your name forever.
[13]For great is your love toward me;
    you have delivered my soul from the depths of
        the grave.[a]

[14]The arrogant are attacking me, O God;
    a band of ruthless men seeks my life—
    men without regard for you.
[15]But you, O Lord, are a compassionate and gracious
        God,
    slow to anger, abounding in love and
        faithfulness.
[16]Turn to me and have mercy on me;
    grant your strength to your servant
    and save the son of your maidservant.[b]
[17]Give me a sign of your goodness,
    that my enemies may see it and be put to
        shame,
    for you, O Lord, have helped me and comforted
        me.

Psalm 87

Of the Sons of Korah. A psalm. A song.

[1]He has set his foundation on the holy mountain;
[2] the Lord loves the gates of Zion
    more than all the dwellings of Jacob.
[3]Glorious things are said of you,
    O city of God: *Selah*

---

[a] 13 Hebrew *Sheol*   [b] 16 Or *save your faithful son*

4"I will record Rahab[a] and Babylon
    among those who acknowledge me—
Philistia too, and Tyre, along with Cush[b]—
    and will say, 'This[c] one was born in Zion.'"

5Indeed, of Zion it will be said,
    "This one and that one were born in her,
    and the Most High himself will establish her."
6The LORD will write in the register of the peoples:
    "This one was born in Zion."   *Selah*
7As they make music they will sing,
    "All my fountains are in you."

Psalm 88

A song. A psalm of the Sons of Korah. For the director of music.
According to *mahalath leannoth*.[d] A *maskil*[e] of Heman the Ezrahite.

1O LORD, the God who saves me,
    day and night I cry out before you.
2May my prayer come before you;
    turn your ear to my cry.

3For my soul is full of trouble
    and my life draws near the grave.[f]
4I am counted among those who go down to the
        pit;
    I am like a man without strength.
5I am set apart with the dead,
    like the slain who lie in the grave,
whom you remember no more,
    who are cut off from your care.

6You have put me in the lowest pit,
    in the darkest depths.
7Your wrath lies heavily upon me;
    you have overwhelmed me with all your waves.
                                            Selah

8You have taken from me my closest friends

a4 A poetic name for Egypt
b4 That is, the upper Nile region
c4 Or "O Rahab and Babylon, / Philistia, Tyre and Cush, / I will record
concerning those who acknowledge me: / 'This
d Title: Possibly a tune, "The Suffering of Affliction"
e Title: Probably a literary or musical term   f3 Hebrew *Sheol*

and have made me repulsive to them.
I am confined and cannot escape;
9   my eyes are dim with grief.

I call to you, O LORD, every day;
    I spread out my hands to you.
10Do you show your wonders to the dead?
    Do those who are dead rise up and praise you?
                                                    Selah

11Is your love declared in the grave,
    your faithfulness in Destruction[a]?
12Are your wonders known in the place of
        darkness,
    or your righteous deeds in the land of oblivion?

13But I cry to you for help, O LORD;
    in the morning my prayer comes before you.
14Why, O LORD, do you reject me
    and hide your face from me?

15From my youth I have been afflicted and close to
        death;
    I have suffered your terrors and am in despair.
16Your wrath has swept over me;
    your terrors have destroyed me.
17All day long they surround me like a flood;
    they have completely engulfed me.
18You have taken my companions and loved ones
        from me;
    the darkness is my closest friend.

Psalm 89

A *maskil*[b] of Ethan the Ezrahite.

1I will sing of the love of the LORD forever;
    with my mouth I will make your faithfulness
        known through all generations.
2I will declare that your love stands firm forever,
    that you established your faithfulness in heaven
        itself.

---

a 11 Hebrew *Abaddon*
b Title: Probably a literary or musical term

³You said, "I have made a covenant with my
      chosen one,
  I have sworn to David my servant,
⁴'I will establish your line forever
  and make your throne firm through all
      generations.' "   *Selah*

⁵The heavens praise your wonders, O LORD,
  your faithfulness too, in the assembly of the
      holy ones.
⁶For who in the skies above can compare with the
      LORD?
  Who is like the LORD among the heavenly
      beings?
⁷In the council of the holy ones God is greatly
      feared;
  he is more awesome than all who surround
      him.
⁸O LORD God Almighty, who is like you?
  You are mighty, O LORD, and your faithfulness
      surrounds you.

⁹You rule over the surging sea;
  when its waves mount up, you still them.
¹⁰You crushed Rahab like one of the slain;
  with your strong arm you scattered your
      enemies.
¹¹The heavens are yours, and yours also the earth;
  you founded the world and all that is in it.
¹²You created the north and the south;
  Tabor and Hermon sing for joy at your name.
¹³Your arm is endued with power;
  your hand is strong, your right hand exalted.

¹⁴Righteousness and justice are the foundation of
      your throne;
  love and faithfulness go before you.
¹⁵Blessed are those who have learned to acclaim
      you,
  who walk in the light of your presence, O
      LORD.
¹⁶They rejoice in your name all day long;
  they exult in your righteousness.

¹⁷For you are their glory and strength,
and by your favor you exalt our horn.^a
¹⁸Indeed, our shield^b belongs to the LORD,
our king to the Holy One of Israel.

¹⁹Once you spoke in a vision,
to your faithful people you said:
"I have bestowed strength on a warrior;
I have exalted a young man from among the
people.
²⁰I have found David my servant;
with my sacred oil I have anointed him.
²¹My hand will sustain him;
surely my arm will strengthen him.
²²No enemy will subject him to tribute;
no wicked man will oppress him.
²³I will crush his foes before him
and strike down his adversaries.
²⁴My faithful love will be with him,
and through my name his horn^c will be exalted.
²⁵I will set his hand over the sea,
his right hand over the rivers.
²⁶He will call out to me, 'You are my Father,
my God, the Rock my Savior.'
²⁷I will also appoint him my firstborn,
the most exalted of the kings of the earth.
²⁸I will maintain my love to him forever,
and my covenant with him will never fail.
²⁹I will establish his line forever,
his throne as long as the heavens endure.

³⁰"If his sons forsake my law
and do not follow my statutes,
³¹if they violate my decrees
and fail to keep my commands,
³²I will punish their sin with the rod,
their iniquity with flogging;
³³but I will not take my love from him,
nor will I ever betray my faithfulness.
³⁴I will not violate my covenant

---

^a 17 *Horn* here symbolizes strong one.   ^b 18 Or *sovereign*
^c 24 *Horn* here symbolizes strength.

or alter what my lips have uttered.
[35]Once for all, I have sworn by my holiness—
   and I will not lie to David—
[36]that his line will continue forever
   and his throne endure before me like the sun;
[37]it will be established forever like the moon,
   the faithful witness in the sky."   *Selah*

[38]But you have rejected, you have spurned,
   you have been very angry with your anointed
      one.
[39]You have renounced the covenant with your
      servant
   and have defiled his crown in the dust.
[40]You have broken through all his walls
   and reduced his strongholds to ruins.
[41]All who pass by have plundered him;
   he has become the scorn of his neighbors.
[42]You have exalted the right hand of his foes;
   you have made all his enemies rejoice.
[43]You have turned back the edge of his sword
   and have not supported him in battle.
[44]You have put an end to his splendor
   and cast his throne to the ground.
[45]You have cut short the days of his youth;
   you have covered him with a mantle of shame.
                                          Selah

[46]How long, O LORD? Will you hide yourself
      forever?
   How long will your wrath burn like fire?
[47]Remember how fleeting is my life.
   For what futility you have created all men!
[48]What man can live and not see death,
   or save himself from the power of the grave[a]?
                                          Selah

[49]O Lord, where is your former great love,
   which in your faithfulness you swore to David?
[50]Remember, Lord, how your servant has[b] been
      mocked,

a 48 Hebrew *Sheol*   b 50 Or *your servants have*

how I bear in my heart the taunts of all the
nations,
⁵¹the taunts with which your enemies have mocked,
O LORD,
with which they have mocked every step of
your anointed one.

⁵²Praise be to the LORD forever!
Amen and Amen.

BOOK IV

Psalms 90-106

Psalm 90

A prayer of Moses the man of God.

¹Lord, you have been our dwelling place
throughout all generations.
²Before the mountains were born
or you brought forth the earth and the world,
from everlasting to everlasting you are God.

³You turn men back to dust,
saying, "Return to dust, O sons of men."
⁴For a thousand years in your sight
are like a day that has just gone by,
or like a watch in the night.
⁵You sweep men away in the sleep of death;
they are like the new grass of the morning—
⁶though in the morning it springs up new,
by evening it is dry and withered.

⁷We are consumed by your anger
and terrified by your indignation.
⁸You have set our iniquities before you,
our secret sins in the light of your presence.
⁹All our days pass away under your wrath;
we finish our years with a moan.
¹⁰The length of our days is seventy years—
or eighty, if we have the strength;

yet their span[a] is but trouble and sorrow,
   for they quickly pass, and we fly away.

11Who knows the power of your anger?
   For your wrath is as great as the fear that is due
     you.
12Teach us to number our days aright,
   that we may gain a heart of wisdom.

13Relent, O LORD! How long will it be?
   Have compassion on your servants.
14Satisfy us in the morning with your unfailing
    love,
   that we may sing for joy and be glad all our
    days.
15Make us glad for as many days as you have
    afflicted us,
   for as many years as we have seen trouble.
16May your deeds be shown to your servants,
   your splendor to their children.

17May the favor of the Lord our God rest upon us;
   establish the work of our hands for us—
   yes, establish the work of our hands.

Psalm 91

1He who dwells in the shelter of the Most High
   will rest in the shadow of the Almighty.[b]
2I will say of the LORD, "He is my refuge and my
    fortress,
   my God, in whom I trust."

3Surely he will save you from the fowler's snare
   and from the deadly pestilence.
4He will cover you with his feathers,
   and under his wings you will find refuge;
   his faithfulness will be your shield and rampart.
5You will not fear the terror of night,
   nor the arrow that flies by day,
6nor the pestilence that stalks in the darkness,
   nor the plague that destroys at midday.

a 10 Or *yet the best of them*   b 1 Hebrew *Shaddai*

⁷A thousand may fall at your side,
ten thousand at your right hand,
but it will not come near you.
⁸You will only observe with your eyes
and see the punishment of the wicked.

⁹If you make the Most High your dwelling—
even the LORD, who is my refuge—
¹⁰then no harm will befall you,
no disaster will come near your tent.
¹¹For he will command his angels concerning you
to guard you in all your ways;
¹²they will lift you up in their hands,
so that you will not strike your foot against a
stone.
¹³You will tread upon the lion and the cobra;
you will trample the great lion and the serpent.

¹⁴"Because he loves me," says the LORD, "I will
rescue him;
I will protect him, for he acknowledges my
name.
¹⁵He will call upon me, and I will answer him;
I will be with him in trouble,
I will deliver him and honor him.
¹⁶With long life will I satisfy him
and show him my salvation."

Psalm 92

A psalm. A song. For the Sabbath day.

¹It is good to praise the LORD
and make music to your name, O Most High,
²to proclaim your love in the morning
and your faithfulness at night,
³to the music of the ten-stringed lyre
and the melody of the harp.

⁴For you make me glad by your deeds, O LORD;
I sing for joy at the works of your hands.
⁵How great are your works, O LORD,
how profound your thoughts!
⁶The senseless man does not know,

fools do not understand,
⁷that though the wicked spring up like grass
    and all evildoers flourish,
 they will be forever destroyed.

⁸But you, O LORD, are exalted forever.

⁹For surely your enemies, O LORD,
    surely your enemies will perish;
    all evildoers will be scattered.
¹⁰You have exalted my horn[a] like that of a wild ox;
    fine oils have been poured upon me.
¹¹My eyes have seen the defeat of my adversaries;
    my ears have heard the rout of my wicked foes.

¹²The righteous will flourish like a palm tree,
    they will grow like a cedar of Lebanon;
¹³planted in the house of the LORD,
    they will flourish in the courts of our God.
¹⁴They will still bear fruit in old age,
    they will stay fresh and green,
¹⁵proclaiming, "The LORD is upright;
    he is my Rock, and there is no wickedness in
        him."

Psalm 93

¹The LORD reigns, he is robed in majesty;
    the LORD is robed in majesty
    and is armed with strength.
 The world is firmly established;
    it cannot be moved.
²Your throne was established long ago;
    you are from all eternity.

³The seas have lifted up, O LORD,
    the seas have lifted up their voice;
    the seas have lifted up their pounding waves.
⁴Mightier than the thunder of the great waters,
    mightier than the breakers of the sea—
    the LORD on high is mighty.

⁵Your statutes stand firm;

a 10 *Horn* here symbolizes strength.

holiness adorns your house
for endless days, O Lord.

Psalm 94

¹O Lord, the God who avenges,
O God who avenges, shine forth.
²Rise up, O Judge of the earth;
pay back to the proud what they deserve.
³How long will the wicked, O Lord,
how long will the wicked be jubilant?

⁴They pour out arrogant words;
all the evildoers are full of boasting.
⁵They crush your people, O Lord;
they oppress your inheritance.
⁶They slay the widow and the alien;
they murder the fatherless.
⁷They say, "The Lord does not see;
the God of Jacob pays no heed."

⁸Take heed, you senseless ones among the people;
you fools, when will you become wise?
⁹Does he who implanted the ear not hear?
Does he who formed the eye not see?
¹⁰Does he who disciplines nations not punish?
Does he who teaches man lack knowledge?
¹¹The Lord knows the thoughts of man;
he knows that they are futile.

¹²Blessed is the man you discipline, O Lord,
the man you teach from your law;
¹³you grant him relief from days of trouble,
till a pit is dug for the wicked.
¹⁴For the Lord will not reject his people;
he will never forsake his inheritance.
¹⁵Judgment will again be founded on righteousness,
and all the upright in heart will follow it.

¹⁶Who will rise up for me against the wicked?
Who will take a stand for me against evildoers?
¹⁷Unless the Lord had given me help,
I would soon have dwelt in the silence of death.
¹⁸When I said, "My foot is slipping,"

your love, O LORD, supported me.
¹⁹When anxiety was great within me,
   your consolation brought joy to my soul.

²⁰Can a corrupt throne be allied with you—
   one that brings on misery by its decrees?
²¹They band together against the righteous
   and condemn the innocent to death.
²²But the LORD has become my fortress,
   and my God the rock in whom I take refuge.
²³He will repay them for their sins
   and destroy them for their wickedness;
   the LORD our God will destroy them.

Psalm 95

¹Come, let us sing for joy to the LORD;
   let us shout aloud to the Rock of our salvation.
²Let us come before him with thanksgiving
   and extol him with music and song.

³For the LORD is the great God,
   the great King above all gods.
⁴In his hand are the depths of the earth,
   and the mountain peaks belong to him.
⁵The sea is his, for he made it,
   and his hands formed the dry land.

⁶Come, let us bow down in worship,
   let us kneel before the LORD our Maker;
⁷for he is our God
   and we are the people of his pasture,
   the flock under his care.

Today, if you hear his voice,
⁸ do not harden your hearts as you did at
     Meribah,[a]
  as you did that day at Massah[b] in the desert,
⁹where your fathers tested and tried me,
   though they had seen what I did.
¹⁰For forty years I was angry with that generation;

---

[a] 8 *Meribah* means *quarreling*.   [b] 8 *Massah* means *testing*.

I said, "They are a people whose hearts go
        astray,
    and they have not known my ways."
[11]So I declared on oath in my anger,
    "They shall never enter my rest."

Psalm 96

[1]Sing to the LORD a new song;
    sing to the LORD, all the earth.
[2]Sing to the LORD, praise his name;
    proclaim his salvation day after day.
[3]Declare his glory among the nations,
    his marvelous deeds among all peoples.

[4]For great is the LORD and most worthy of praise;
    he is to be feared above all gods.
[5]For all the gods of the nations are idols,
    but the LORD made the heavens.
[6]Splendor and majesty are before him;
    strength and glory are in his sanctuary.

[7]Ascribe to the LORD, O families of nations,
    ascribe to the LORD glory and strength.
[8]Ascribe to the LORD the glory due his name;
    bring an offering and come into his courts.
[9]Worship the LORD in the splendor of his[a]
        holiness;
    tremble before him, all the earth.

[10]Say among the nations, "The LORD reigns."
    The world is firmly established, it cannot be
        moved;
    he will judge the peoples with equity.
[11]Let the heavens rejoice, let the earth be glad;
    let the sea resound, and all that is in it;
[12]   let the fields be jubilant, and everything in them.
    Then all the trees of the forest will sing for joy;
[13]   they will sing before the LORD, for he comes,
    he comes to judge the earth.
    He will judge the world in righteousness
        and the peoples in his truth.

[a]9 Or LORD with the splendor of

Psalm 97

¹The LORD reigns, let the earth be glad;
  let the distant shores rejoice.

²Clouds and thick darkness surround him;
  righteousness and justice are the foundation of
    his throne.
³Fire goes before him
  and consumes his foes on every side.
⁴His lightning lights up the world;
  the earth sees and trembles.
⁵The mountains melt like wax before the LORD,
  before the Lord of all the earth.
⁶The heavens proclaim his righteousness,
  and all the peoples see his glory.

⁷All who worship images are put to shame,
  those who boast in idols—
    worship him, all you gods!

⁸Zion hears and rejoices
  and the villages of Judah are glad
  because of your judgments, O LORD.
⁹For you, O LORD, are the Most High over all the
    earth;
  you are exalted far above all gods.

¹⁰Let those who love the LORD hate evil,
  for he guards the lives of his faithful ones
  and delivers them from the hand of the
    wicked.
¹¹Light is shed upon the righteous
  and joy on the upright in heart.
¹²Rejoice in the LORD, you who are righteous,
  and praise his holy name.

Psalm 98

A psalm.

¹Sing to the LORD a new song,
  for he has done marvelous things;
his right hand and his holy arm

have worked salvation for him.
2The LORD has made his salvation known
  and revealed his righteousness to the nations.
3He has remembered his love
  and his faithfulness to the house of Israel;
all the ends of the earth have seen
  the salvation of our God.

4Shout for joy to the LORD, all the earth,
  burst into jubilant song with music;
5make music to the LORD with the harp,
  with the harp and the sound of singing,
6with trumpets and the blast of the ram's horn—
  shout for joy before the LORD, the King.

7Let the sea resound, and all that is in it,
  the world, and all who live in it.
8Let the rivers clap their hands,
  let the mountains sing together for joy;
9let them sing before the LORD,
  for he comes to judge the earth.
He will judge the world in righteousness
  and the peoples with equity.

Psalm 99

1The LORD reigns,
  let the nations tremble;
he sits enthroned between the cherubim,
  let the earth shake.
2Great is the LORD in Zion;
  he is exalted over all the nations.
3Let them praise your great and awesome name—
  he is holy.

4The King is mighty, he loves justice—
  you have established equity;
in Jacob you have done
  what is just and right.
5Exalt the LORD our God
  and worship at his footstool;
  he is holy.

6Moses and Aaron were among his priests,

Samuel was among those who called on his
    name;
they called on the LORD
    and he answered them.
[7]He spoke to them from the pillar of cloud;
    they kept his statutes and the decrees he gave
    them.

[8]O LORD our God,
    you answered them;
you were to Israel[a] a forgiving God,
    though you punished their misdeeds.[b]
[9]Exalt the LORD our God
    and worship at his holy mountain,
    for the LORD our God is holy.

Psalm 100

A psalm. For giving thanks.

[1]Shout for joy to the LORD, all the earth.
[2] Serve the LORD with gladness;
    come before him with joyful songs.
[3]Know that the LORD is God.
    It is he who made us, and we are his[c];
    we are his people, the sheep of his pasture.

[4]Enter his gates with thanksgiving
    and his courts with praise;
    give thanks to him and praise his name.
[5]For the LORD is good and his love endures forever;
    his faithfulness continues through all
    generations.

Psalm 101

Of David. A psalm.

[1]I will sing of your love and justice;
    to you, O LORD, I will sing praise.
[2]I will be careful to lead a blameless life—
    when will you come to me?

a 8 Hebrew *them*   b 8 Or / *an avenger of the wrongs done to them*
c 3 Or *and not we ourselves*

I will walk in my house
with blameless heart.
[3]I will set before my eyes
no vile thing.

The deeds of faithless men I hate;
they will not cling to me.
[4]Men of perverse heart shall be far from me;
I will have nothing to do with evil.

[5]Whoever slanders his neighbor in secret,
him will I put to silence;
whoever has haughty eyes and a proud heart,
him will I not endure.

[6]My eyes will be on the faithful in the land,
that they may dwell with me;
he whose walk is blameless
will minister to me.

[7]No one who practices deceit
will dwell in my house;
no one who speaks falsely
will stand in my presence.

[8]Every morning I will put to silence
all the wicked in the land;
I will cut off every evildoer
from the city of the LORD.

Psalm 102

*A prayer of an afflicted man. When he is faint and pours out his
lament before the LORD.*

[1]Hear my prayer, O LORD;
let my cry for help come to you.
[2]Do not hide your face from me
when I am in distress.
Turn your ear to me;
when I call, answer me quickly.

[3]For my days vanish like smoke;
my bones burn like glowing embers.
[4]My heart is blighted and withered like grass;
I forget to eat my food.

5Because of my loud groaning
  I am reduced to skin and bones.
6I am like a desert owl,
  like an owl among the ruins.
7I lie awake; I have become
  like a bird alone on a housetop.
8All day long my enemies taunt me;
  those who rail against me use my name as a
    curse.
9For I eat ashes as my food
  and mingle my drink with tears
10because of your great wrath,
  for you have taken me up and thrown me aside.
11My days are like the evening shadow;
  I wither away like grass.

12But you, O Lord, sit enthroned forever;
  your renown endures through all generations.
13You will arise and have compassion on Zion,
  for it is time to show favor to her;
  the appointed time has come.
14For her stones are dear to your servants;
  her very dust moves them to pity.
15The nations will fear the name of the Lord,
  all the kings of the earth will revere your glory.
16For the Lord will rebuild Zion
  and appear in his glory.
17He will respond to the prayer of the destitute;
  he will not despise their plea.

18Let this be written for a future generation,
  that a people not yet created may praise the
    Lord:
19"The Lord looked down from his sanctuary on
    high,
  from heaven he viewed the earth,
20to hear the groans of the prisoners
  and release those condemned to death."
21So the name of the Lord will be declared in Zion
  and his praise in Jerusalem
22when the peoples and the kingdoms
  assemble to worship the Lord.

²³In the course of my life[a] he broke my strength;
 he cut short my days.
²⁴So I said:
 "Do not take me away, O my God, in the midst
  of my days;
 your years go on through all generations.
²⁵In the beginning you laid the foundations of the
  earth,
 and the heavens are the work of your hands.
²⁶They will perish, but you remain;
 they will all wear out like a garment.
Like clothing you will change them
 and they will be discarded.
²⁷But you remain the same,
 and your years will never end.
²⁸The children of your servants will live in your
  presence;
 their descendants will be established before
  you."

Psalm 103

Of David.

¹Praise the LORD, O my soul;
 all my inmost being, praise his holy name.
²Praise the LORD, O my soul,
 and forget not all his benefits.

³He forgives all my[b] sins
 and heals all my diseases;
⁴he redeems my life from the pit
 and crowns me with love and compassion.
⁵He satisfies my desires with good things,
 so that my youth is renewed like the eagle's
⁶The LORD works righteousness
 and justice for all the oppressed.
⁷He made known his ways to Moses,
 his deeds to the people of Israel:
⁸The LORD is compassionate and gracious,
 slow to anger, abounding in love.

ᵃ 23 Or *By his power*
ᵇ 3 Hebrew *your* (referring to *my soul*); also in verses 3b-5

⁹He will not always accuse,
  nor will he harbor his anger forever;
¹⁰he does not treat us as our sins deserve
  or repay us according to our iniquities.
¹¹For as high as the heavens are above the earth,
  so great is his love for those who fear him;
¹²as far as the east is from the west,
  so far has he removed our transgressions from
    us.
¹³As a father has compassion on his children,
  so the LORD has compassion on those who fear
    him;
¹⁴for he knows how we are formed,
  he remembers that we are dust.
¹⁵As for man, his days are like grass,
  he flourishes like a flower of the field;
¹⁶the wind blows over it and it is gone,
  and its place remembers it no more.
¹⁷But from everlasting to everlasting
  the LORD's love is with those who fear him,
  and his righteousness with their children's
    children—
¹⁸with those who keep his covenant
  and remember to obey his precepts.

¹⁹The LORD has established his throne in heaven,
  and his kingdom rules over all.

²⁰Praise the LORD, you his angels,
  you mighty ones who do his bidding,
  who obey his word.
²¹Praise the LORD, all his heavenly hosts,
  you his servants who do his will.
²²Praise the LORD, all his works
  everywhere in his dominion.

Praise the LORD, O my soul.

Psalm 104

¹Praise the LORD, O my soul.

O LORD my God, you are very great;
  you are clothed with splendor and majesty.

²He wraps himself in light as with a garment;
  he stretches out the heavens like a tent
³ and lays the beams of his upper chambers on
      their waters.
 He makes the clouds his chariot
    and rides on the wings of the wind.
⁴He makes winds his messengers,^a
  flames of fire his servants.

⁵He set the earth on its foundations;
  it can never be moved.
⁶You covered it with the deep as with a garment;
  the waters stood above the mountains.
⁷But at your rebuke the waters fled,
  at the sound of your thunder they took to flight;
⁸they flowed over the mountains,
    they went down into the valleys,
    to the place you assigned for them.
⁹You set a boundary they cannot cross;
  never again will they cover the earth.

¹⁰He makes springs pour water into the ravines;
  it flows between the mountains.
¹¹They give water to all the beasts of the field;
  the wild donkeys quench their thirst.
¹²The birds of the air nest by the waters;
  they sing among the branches.
¹³He waters the mountains from his upper
      chambers;
  the earth is satisfied by the fruit of his work.
¹⁴He makes grass grow for the cattle,
    and plants for man to cultivate—
    bringing forth food from the earth:
¹⁵wine that gladdens the heart of man,
    oil to make his face shine,
    and bread that sustains his heart.
¹⁶The trees of the LORD are well watered,
  the cedars of Lebanon that he planted.
¹⁷There the birds make their nests;
  the stork has its home in the pine trees.
¹⁸The high mountains belong to the wild goats;

^a 4 Or *angels*

the crags are a refuge for the coneys.[a]

19The moon marks off the seasons,
    and the sun knows when to go down.
20You bring darkness, it becomes night,
    and all the beasts of the forest prowl.
21The lions roar for their prey
    and seek their food from God.
22The sun rises, and they steal away;
    they return and lie down in their dens.
23Then man goes out to his work,
    to his labor until evening.

24How many are your works, O Lord!
    In wisdom you made them all;
    the earth is full of your creatures.
25There is the sea, vast and spacious,
    teeming with creatures beyond number—
    living things both large and small.
26There the ships go to and fro,
    and the leviathan, which you formed to frolic
        there.

27These all look to you
    to give them their food at the proper time.
28When you give it to them,
    they gather it up;
  when you open your hand,
    they are satisfied with good things.
29When you hide your face,
    they are terrified;
  when you take away their breath,
    they die and return to the dust.
30When you send your Spirit,
    they are created,
    and you renew the face of the earth.

31May the glory of the Lord endure forever;
    may the Lord rejoice in his works.
32He looks at the earth, and it trembles;
    he touches the mountains, and they smoke.

---

a 18 That is, the hyrax or rock badger

³³I will sing to the LORD all my life;
  I will sing praise to my God as long as I live.
³⁴May my meditation be pleasing to him,
  as I rejoice in the LORD.
³⁵But may sinners vanish from the earth
  and the wicked be no more.

Praise the LORD, O my soul.

Praise the LORD.^a

Psalm 105

¹Give thanks to the LORD, call on his name;
  make known among the nations what he has
    done.
²Sing to him, sing praise to him;
  tell of all his wonderful acts.
³Glory in his holy name;
  let the hearts of those who seek the LORD
    rejoice.
⁴Look to the LORD and his strength;
  seek his face always.
⁵Remember the wonders he has done,
  his miracles, and the judgments he pronounced,
⁶O descendants of Abraham his servant,
  O sons of Jacob, his chosen ones.

⁷He is the LORD our God;
  his judgments are in all the earth.
⁸He remembers his covenant forever,
  the word he commanded, for a thousand
    generations,
⁹the covenant he made with Abraham,
  the oath he swore to Isaac.
¹⁰He confirmed it to Jacob as a decree,
  to Israel as an everlasting covenant:
¹¹"To you I will give the land of Canaan
  as the portion you will inherit."

¹²When they were but few in number,
  few indeed, and strangers in it,

^a 35 Hebrew *Hallelu Yah*

¹³they wandered from nation to nation,
  from one kingdom to another.
¹⁴He allowed no one to oppress them;
  for their sake he rebuked kings:
¹⁵"Do not touch my anointed ones;
  do my prophets no harm."

¹⁶He called down famine on the land
  and destroyed all their supplies of food;
¹⁷and he sent a man before them—
  Joseph, sold as a slave.
¹⁸They bruised his feet with shackles,
  his neck was put in irons,
¹⁹till what he foretold came to pass,
  till the word of the LORD proved him true.
²⁰The king sent and released him,
  the ruler of peoples set him free.
²¹He made him master of his household,
  ruler over all he possessed,
²²to discipline his princes as he pleased
  and teach his elders wisdom.

²³Then Israel entered Egypt;
  Jacob lived as an alien in the land of Ham.
²⁴The LORD made his people very fruitful;
  he made them too numerous for their foes,
²⁵whose hearts he turned to hate his people,
  to conspire against his servants.
²⁶He sent Moses his servant,
  and Aaron, whom he had chosen.
²⁷They performed his miraculous signs among them,
  his wonders in the land of Ham.
²⁸He sent darkness and made the land dark—
  for had they not rebelled against his words?
²⁹He turned their waters into blood,
  causing their fish to die.
³⁰Their land teemed with frogs,
  which went up into the bedrooms of their
      rulers.
³¹He spoke, and there came swarms of flies,
  and gnats throughout their country.
³²He turned their rain into hail,

with lightning throughout their land;
33he struck down their vines and fig trees
   and shattered the trees of their country.
34He spoke, and the locusts came,
   grasshoppers without number;
35they ate up every green thing in their land,
   ate up the produce of their soil.
36Then he struck down all the firstborn in their
      land,
   the firstfruits of all their manhood.

37He brought out Israel, laden with silver and gold,
   and from among their tribes no one faltered.
38Egypt was glad when they left,
   because dread of Israel had fallen on them.
39He spread out a cloud as a covering,
   and a fire to give light at night.
40They asked, and he brought them quail
   and satisfied them with the bread of heaven.
41He opened the rock, and water gushed out;
   like a river it flowed in the desert.
42For he remembered his holy promise
   given to his servant Abraham.
43He brought out his people with rejoicing,
   his chosen ones with shouts of joy;
44he gave them the lands of the nations,
   and they fell heir to what others had toiled
      for—
45that they might keep his precepts
   and observe his laws.

Praise the LORD.[a]

Psalm 106

1Praise the LORD.[b]

Give thanks to the LORD, for he is good;
   his love endures forever.
2Who can proclaim the mighty acts of the LORD
   or fully declare his praise?

a 45 Hebrew *Hallelu Yah*
b 1 Hebrew *Hallelu Yah*; also in verse 48

³Blessed are they who maintain justice,
  who constantly do what is right.
⁴Remember me, O LORD, when you show favor to
      your people,
  come to my aid when you save them,
⁵that I may enjoy the prosperity of your chosen
      ones,
  that I may share in the joy of your nation
  and join your inheritance in giving praise.

⁶We have sinned, even as our fathers did;
  we have done wrong and acted wickedly.
⁷When our fathers were in Egypt,
  they gave no thought to your miracles;
they did not remember your many kindnesses,
  and they rebelled by the sea, the Red Sea.ᵃ
⁸Yet he saved them for his name's sake,
  to make his mighty power known.
⁹He rebuked the Red Sea, and it dried up;
  he led them through the depths as through a
      desert.
¹⁰He saved them from the hand of the foe;
  from the hand of the enemy he redeemed them.
¹¹The waters covered their adversaries;
  not one of them survived.
¹²Then they believed his promises
  and sang his praise.

¹³But they soon forgot what he had done
  and did not wait for his counsel.
¹⁴In the desert they gave in to their craving;
  in the wasteland they put God to the test.
¹⁵So he gave them what they asked for,
  but sent a wasting disease upon them.

¹⁶In the camp they grew envious of Moses
  and of Aaron, who was consecrated to the
      LORD.
¹⁷The earth opened up and swallowed Dathan;
  it buried the company of Abiram.

ᵃ7 Hebrew *Yam Suph;* that is, Sea of Reeds; also in verses 9 and
22

¹⁸Fire blazed among their followers;
a flame consumed the wicked.

¹⁹At Horeb they made a calf
and worshiped an idol cast from metal.
²⁰They exchanged their Glory
for an image of a bull, which eats grass.
²¹They forgot the God who saved them,
who had done great things in Egypt,
²²miracles in the land of Ham
and awesome deeds by the Red Sea.
²³So he said he would destroy them—
had not Moses, his chosen one,
stood in the breach before him
to keep his wrath from destroying them.

²⁴Then they despised the pleasant land;
they did not believe his promise.
²⁵They grumbled in their tents
and did not obey the LORD.
²⁶So he swore to them with uplifted hand
that he would make them fall in the desert,
²⁷make their descendants fall among the nations
and scatter them throughout the lands.

²⁸They yoked themselves to the Baal of Peor
and ate sacrifices offered to lifeless gods;
²⁹they provoked the LORD to anger by their wicked
deeds,
and a plague broke out among them.
³⁰But Phinehas stood up and intervened,
and the plague was checked.
³¹This was credited to him as righteousness
for endless generations to come.

³²By the waters of Meribah they angered the LORD,
and trouble came to Moses because of them;
³³for they rebelled against the Spirit of God,
and rash words came from Moses' lips.ᵃ

³⁴They did not destroy the peoples
as the LORD had commanded them,

ᵃ 33 Or *against his spirit, / and rash words came from his lips*

³⁵but they mingled with the nations
and adopted their customs.
³⁶They worshiped their idols,
which became a snare to them.
³⁷They sacrificed their sons
and their daughters to demons.
³⁸They shed innocent blood,
the blood of their sons and daughters,
whom they sacrificed to the idols of Canaan,
and the land was desecrated by their blood.
³⁹They defiled themselves by what they did;
by their deeds they prostituted themselves.

⁴⁰Therefore the LORD was angry with his people
and abhorred his inheritance.
⁴¹He handed them over to the nations,
and their foes ruled over them.
⁴²Their enemies oppressed them
and subjected them to their power.
⁴³Many times he delivered them,
but they were bent on rebellion
and they wasted away in their sin.

⁴⁴But he took note of their distress
when he heard their cry;
⁴⁵for their sake he remembered his covenant
and out of his great love he relented.
⁴⁶He caused them to be pitied
by all who held them captive.

⁴⁷Save us, O LORD our God,
and gather us from the nations,
that we may give thanks to your holy name
and glory in your praise.

⁴⁸Praise be to the LORD, the God of Israel,
from everlasting to everlasting.
Let all the people say, "Amen!"

Praise the LORD.

BOOK V

Psalms 107-150

Psalm 107

¹Give thanks to the LORD, for he is good;
　　his love endures forever.
²Let the redeemed of the LORD say this—
　　those he redeemed from the hand of the foe,
³those he gathered from the lands,
　　from east and west, from north and south.ª

⁴Some wandered in desert wastelands,
　　finding no way to a city where they could
　　　　settle.
⁵They were hungry and thirsty,
　　and their lives ebbed away.
⁶Then they cried out to the LORD in their trouble,
　　and he delivered them from their distress.
⁷He led them by a straight way
　　to a city where they could settle.
⁸Let them give thanks to the LORD for his unfailing
　　　　love
　　and his wonderful deeds for men,
⁹for he satisfies the thirsty
　　and fills the hungry with good things.

¹⁰Some sat in darkness and the deepest gloom,
　　prisoners suffering in iron chains,
¹¹for they had rebelled against the words of God
　　and despised the counsel of the Most High.
¹²So he subjected them to bitter labor;
　　they stumbled, and there was no one to help.
¹³Then they cried to the LORD in their trouble,
　　and he saved them from their distress.
¹⁴He brought them out of darkness and the deepest
　　　　gloom
　　and broke away their chains.
¹⁵Let them give thanks to the LORD for his unfailing
　　　　love
　　and his wonderful deeds for men,

ª3 Hebrew *north and the sea*

¹⁶for he breaks down gates of bronze
    and cuts through bars of iron.

¹⁷Some became fools through their rebellious ways
    and suffered affliction because of their
        iniquities.
¹⁸They loathed all food
    and drew near the gates of death.
¹⁹Then they cried to the LORD in their trouble,
    and he saved them from their distress.
²⁰He sent forth his word and healed them;
    he rescued them from the grave.
²¹Let them give thanks to the LORD for his unfailing
        love
    and his wonderful deeds for men.
²²Let them sacrifice thank offerings
    and tell of his works with songs of joy.

²³Others went out on the sea in ships;
    they were merchants on the mighty waters.
²⁴They saw the works of the LORD,
    his wonderful deeds in the deep.
²⁵For he spoke and stirred up a tempest
    that lifted high the waves.
²⁶They mounted up to the heavens and went down
        to the depths;
    in their peril their courage melted away.
²⁷They reeled and staggered like drunken men;
    they were at their wits' end.
²⁸Then they cried out to the LORD in their trouble,
    and he brought them out of their distress.
²⁹He stilled the storm to a whisper;
    the waves of the sea were hushed.
³⁰They were glad when it grew calm,
    and he guided them to their desired haven.
³¹Let them give thanks to the LORD for his unfailing
        love
    and his wonderful deeds for men.
³²Let them exalt him in the assembly of the people
    and praise him in the council of the elders.

³³He turned rivers into a desert,
    flowing springs into thirsty ground,

³⁴and fruitful land into a salt waste,
   because of the wickedness of those who lived
      there.
³⁵He turned the desert into pools of water
   and the parched ground into flowing springs;
³⁶there he brought the hungry to live,
   and they founded a city where they could settle.
³⁷They sowed fields and planted vineyards
   that yielded a fruitful harvest;
³⁸he blessed them, and their numbers greatly
      increased,
   and he did not let their herds diminish.

³⁹Then their numbers decreased, and they were
      humbled
   by oppression, calamity and sorrow;
⁴⁰he who pours contempt on nobles
   made them wander in a trackless waste.
⁴¹But he lifted the needy out of their affliction
   and increased their families like flocks.
⁴²The upright see and rejoice,
   but all the wicked shut their mouths.

⁴³Whoever is wise, let him heed these things
   and consider the great love of the LORD.

Psalm 108

A song. A psalm of David.

¹My heart is steadfast, O God;
   I will sing and make music with all my soul.
²Awake, harp and lyre!
   I will awaken the dawn.
³I will praise you, O LORD, among the nations;
   I will sing of you among the peoples.
⁴For great is your love, higher than the heavens;
   your faithfulness reaches to the skies.
⁵Be exalted, O God, above the heavens,
   and let your glory be over all the earth.

⁶Save us and help us with your right hand,
   that those you love may be delivered.
⁷God has spoken from his sanctuary:

"In triumph I will parcel out Shechem
and measure off the Valley of Succoth.
8Gilead is mine, Manasseh is mine;
Ephraim is my helmet,
Judah my scepter.
9Moab is my washbasin,
upon Edom I toss my sandal;
over Philistia I shout in triumph."

10Who will bring me to the fortified city?
Who will lead me to Edom?
11Is it not you, O God, you who have rejected us
and no longer go out with our armies?
12Give us aid against the enemy,
for the help of man is worthless.
13With God we will gain the victory,
and he will trample down our enemies.

Psalm 109

For the director of music. Of David. A psalm.

1O God, whom I praise,
do not remain silent,
2for wicked and deceitful men
have opened their mouths against me;
they have spoken against me with lying
tongues.
3With words of hatred they surround me;
they attack me without cause.
4In return for my friendship they accuse me,
but I am a man of prayer.
5They repay me evil for good,
and hatred for my friendship.

6Appointa an evil manb to oppose him;
let an accuserc stand at his right hand.
7When he is tried, let him be found guilty,
and may his prayers condemn him.
8May his days be few;

a 6 Or They say: "Appoint (with quotation marks at the end of
verse 19)
b 6 Or the Evil One   c 6 Or let Satan

may another take his place of leadership.
⁹May his children be fatherless
    and his wife a widow.
¹⁰May his children be wandering beggars;
    may they be driven^a from their ruined homes.
¹¹May a creditor seize all he has;
    may strangers plunder the fruits of his labor.
¹²May no one extend kindness to him
    or take pity on his fatherless children.
¹³May his descendants be cut off,
    their names blotted out from the next
        generation.
¹⁴May the iniquity of his fathers be remembered
      before the LORD;
    may the sin of his mother never be blotted out.
¹⁵May their sins always remain before the LORD,
    that he may cut off the memory of them from
      the earth.

¹⁶For he never thought of doing a kindness,
    but hounded to death the poor
    and the needy and the brokenhearted.
¹⁷He loved to pronounce a curse—
    may it^b come on him;
 he found no pleasure in blessing—
    may it be^c far from him.
¹⁸He wore cursing as his garment;
    it entered into his body like water,
    into his bones like oil.
¹⁹May it be like a cloak wrapped about him,
    like a belt tied forever around him.

²⁰May this be the LORD's payment to my accusers,
    to those who speak evil of me.
²¹But you, O Sovereign LORD,
    deal well with me for your name's sake;
    out of the goodness of your love, deliver me.

²²For I am poor and needy,
    and my heart is wounded within me.
²³I fade away like an evening shadow;

---

^{a} 10 Septuagint; Hebrew *sought* ^{b} 17 Or *curse, / and it has*
^{c} 17 Or *blessing, / and it is*

I am shaken off like a locust.
24My knees give way from fasting;
      my body is thin and gaunt.
25I am an object of scorn to my accusers;
      when they see me, they shake their heads.

26Help me, O LORD my God;
      save me in accordance with your love.
27Let them know that it is your hand,
      that you, O LORD, have done it.
28They may curse, but you will bless;
      when they attack they will be put to shame,
      but your servant will rejoice.
29My accusers will be clothed with disgrace
      and wrapped in shame as in a cloak.

30With my mouth I will greatly extol the LORD;
      in the great throng I will praise him.
31For he stands at the right hand of the needy one,
      to save his life from those who condemn him.

Psalm 110

Of David. A psalm.

1The LORD says to my Lord:
   "Sit at my right hand
until I make your enemies
   a footstool for your feet."

2The LORD will extend your mighty scepter from
      Zion;
   rule in the midst of your enemies.
3Your troops will be willing
   on your day of battle.
Arrayed in holy majesty,
   from the womb of the dawn
   you will receive the dew of your youth.a

4The LORD has sworn
   and will not change his mind:
"You are a priest forever,
   in the order of Melchizedek."

a 3 Or / your young men will come to you like the dew

⁵The Lord is at your right hand;
    he will crush kings on the day of his wrath.
⁶He will judge the nations, heaping up the dead
    and crushing the rulers of the whole earth.
⁷He will drink from a brook beside the way[a];
    therefore, he will lift up his head.

Psalm 111[b]

¹Praise the LORD.[c]

I will extol the LORD with all my heart
    in the council of the upright and in the
        assembly.

²Great are the works of the LORD;
    they are pondered by all who delight in them.
³Glorious and majestic are his deeds,
    and his righteousness endures forever.
⁴He has caused his wonders to be remembered;
    the LORD is gracious and compassionate.
⁵He provides food for those who fear him;
    he remembers his covenant forever.
⁶He has shown his people the power of his works,
    giving them the lands of other nations.
⁷The works of his hands are faithful and just;
    all his precepts are trustworthy.
⁸They are steadfast for ever and ever,
    done in faithfulness and uprightness.
⁹He provided redemption for his people;
    he ordained his covenant forever—
    holy and awesome is his name.

¹⁰The fear of the LORD is the beginning of wisdom;
    all who follow his precepts have good
        understanding.
    To him belongs eternal praise.

---

a7 Or / *The One who grants succession will set him in authority*
b This psalm is an acrostic poem, the lines of which begin with
the successive letters of the Hebrew alphabet.
c1 Hebrew *Hallelu Yah*

Psalm 112[a]

[1]Praise the LORD.[b]

Blessed is the man who fears the LORD,
  who finds great delight in his commands.
[2]His children will be mighty in the land;
  each generation of the upright will be blessed.
[3]Wealth and riches are in his house,
  and his righteousness endures forever.
[4]Even in darkness light dawns for the upright,
  for the gracious and compassionate and
    righteous man.[c]
[5]Good will come to him who is generous and lends
    freely,
  who conducts his affairs with justice.
[6]Surely he will never be shaken;
  a righteous man will be remembered forever.
[7]He will have no fear of bad news;
  his heart is steadfast, trusting in the LORD.
[8]His heart is secure, he will have no fear;
  in the end he will look in triumph on his foes.
[9]He has scattered abroad his gifts to the poor,
  his righteousness endures forever;
  his horn[d] will be lifted high in honor.

[10]The wicked man will see and be vexed,
  he will gnash his teeth and waste away;
  the longings of the wicked will come to
    nothing.

Psalm 113

[1]Praise the LORD.[e]

Praise, O servants of the LORD,
  praise the name of the LORD.
[2]Let the name of the LORD be praised,

[a] This psalm is an acrostic poem, the lines of which begin with
the successive letters of the Hebrew alphabet.
[b] 1 Hebrew Hallelu Yah
[c] 4 Or / for the LORD, is gracious and compassionate and righteous
[d] 9 Horn here symbolizes dignity.
[e] 1 Hebrew Hallelu Yah; also in verse 9

both now and forevermore.
3From the rising of the sun to the place where it
sets
the name of the LORD is to be praised.

4The LORD is exalted over all the nations,
his glory above the heavens.
5Who is like the LORD our God,
the One who sits enthroned on high,
6who stoops down to look
on the heavens and the earth?

7He raises the poor from the dust
and lifts the needy from the ash heap;
8he seats them with princes,
with the princes of their people.
9He settles the barren woman in her home
as a happy mother of children.

Praise the LORD.

Psalm 114

1When Israel came out of Egypt,
the house of Jacob from a people of foreign
tongue,
2Judah became God's sanctuary,
Israel his dominion.

3The sea looked and fled,
the Jordan turned back;
4the mountains skipped like rams,
the hills like lambs.

5Why was it, O sea, that you fled,
O Jordan, that you turned back,
6you mountains, that you skipped like rams,
you hills, like lambs?

7Tremble, O earth, at the presence of the Lord,
at the presence of the God of Jacob,
8who turned the rock into a pool,
the hard rock into springs of water.

Psalm 115

¹Not to us, O Lord, not to us
  but to your name be the glory,
  because of your love and faithfulness.

²Why do the nations say,
  "Where is their God?"
³Our God is in heaven;
  he does whatever pleases him.
⁴But their idols are silver and gold,
  made by the hands of men.
⁵They have mouths, but cannot speak,
  eyes, but they cannot see;
⁶they have ears, but cannot hear,
  noses, but they cannot smell;
⁷they have hands, but cannot feel,
  feet, but they cannot walk;
  nor can they utter a sound with their throats.
⁸Those who make them will be like them,
  and so will all who trust in them.

⁹O house of Israel, trust in the Lord—
  he is their help and shield.
¹⁰O house of Aaron, trust in the Lord—
  he is their help and shield.
¹¹You who fear him, trust in the Lord—
  he is their help and shield.

¹²The Lord remembers us and will bless us:
  He will bless the house of Israel,
  he will bless the house of Aaron,
¹³he will bless those who fear the Lord—
  small and great alike.

¹⁴May the Lord make you increase,
  both you and your children.
¹⁵May you be blessed by the Lord,
  the Maker of heaven and earth.

¹⁶The highest heavens belong to the Lord,
  but the earth he has given to man.
¹⁷It is not the dead who praise the Lord,
  those who go down to silence;

¹⁸it is we who extol the LORD,
   both now and forevermore.

Praise the LORD.ᵃ

Psalm 116

¹I love the LORD, for he heard my voice;
   he heard my cry for mercy.
²Because he turned his ear to me,
   I will call on him as long as I live.

³The cords of death entangled me,
   the anguish of the graveᵇ came upon me;
   I was overcome by trouble and sorrow.
⁴Then I called on the name of the LORD:
   "O LORD, save me!"

⁵The LORD is gracious and righteous;
   our God is full of compassion.
⁶The LORD protects the simplehearted;
   when I was in great need, he saved me.

⁷Be at rest once more, O my soul,
   for the LORD has been good to you.

⁸For you, O LORD, have delivered my soul from
      death,
   my eyes from tears,
   my feet from stumbling,
⁹that I may walk before the LORD
   in the land of the living.
¹⁰I believed; thereforeᶜ I said,
   "I am greatly afflicted."
¹¹And in my dismay I said,
   "All men are liars."

¹²How can I repay the LORD
   for all his goodness to me?
¹³I will lift up the cup of salvation
   and call on the name of the LORD.
¹⁴I will fulfill my vows to the LORD

ᵃ18 Hebrew *Hallelu Yah*   ᵇ3 Hebrew *Sheol*
ᶜ10 Or *believed even when*

in the presence of all his people.

15Precious in the sight of the LORD
is the death of his saints.
16O LORD, truly I am your servant;
I am your servant, the son of your
maidservant[a];
you have freed me from my chains.

17I will sacrifice a thank offering to you
and call on the name of the LORD.
18I will fulfill my vows to the LORD
in the presence of all his people,
19in the courts of the house of the LORD—
in your midst, O Jerusalem.

Praise the LORD.[b]

Psalm 117

1Praise the LORD, all you nations;
extol him, all you peoples.
2For great is his love toward us,
and the faithfulness of the LORD endures
forever.

Praise the LORD.[b]

Psalm 118

1Give thanks to the LORD, for he is good;
his love endures forever.

2Let Israel say:
"His love endures forever."
3Let the house of Aaron say:
"His love endures forever."
4Let those who fear the LORD say:
"His love endures forever."

5In my anguish I cried to the LORD,
and he answered by setting me free.
6The LORD is with me; I will not be afraid.
What can man do to me?

a 16 Or *servant, your faithful son*   b 19,2 Hebrew *Hallelu Yah*

⁷The LORD is with me; he is my helper.
  I will look in triumph on my enemies.

⁸It is better to take refuge in the LORD
  than to trust in man.
⁹It is better to take refuge in the LORD
  than to trust in princes.

¹⁰All the nations surrounded me,
  but in the name of the LORD I cut them off.
¹¹They surrounded me on every side,
  but in the name of the LORD I cut them off.
¹²They swarmed around me like bees,
  but they died out as quickly as burning thorns;
  in the name of the LORD I cut them off.

¹³I was pushed back and about to fall,
  but the LORD helped me.
¹⁴The LORD is my strength and my song;
  he has become my salvation.

¹⁵Shouts of joy and victory
  resound in the tents of the righteous:
 "The LORD's right hand has done mighty things!
¹⁶   The LORD's right hand is lifted high;
  the LORD's right hand has done mighty things!"

¹⁷I will not die but live,
  and will proclaim what the LORD has done.
¹⁸The LORD has chastened me severely,
  but he has not given me over to death.

¹⁹Open for me the gates of righteousness;
  I will enter and give thanks to the LORD.
²⁰This is the gate of the LORD
  through which the righteous may enter.
²¹I will give you thanks, for you answered me;
  you have become my salvation.

²²The stone the builders rejected
  has become the capstone;
²³the LORD has done this,
  and it is marvelous in our eyes.
²⁴This is the day the LORD has made;
  let us rejoice and be glad in it.

[25]O Lord, save us;
   O Lord, grant us success.
[26]Blessed is he who comes in the name of the Lord.
   From the house of the Lord we bless you.[a]
[27]The Lord is God,
   and he has made his light shine upon us.
With boughs in hand, join in the festal procession
   up[b] to the horns of the altar.

[28]You are my God, and I will give you thanks;
   you are my God, and I will exalt you.

[29]Give thanks to the Lord, for he is good;
   his love endures forever.

Psalm 119[c]

א Aleph

[1]Blessed are they whose ways are blameless,
   who walk according to the law of the Lord.
[2]Blessed are they who keep his statutes
   and seek him with all their heart.
[3]They do nothing wrong;
   they walk in his ways.
[4]You have laid down precepts
   that are to be fully obeyed.
[5]Oh, that my ways were steadfast
   in obeying your decrees!
[6]Then I would not be put to shame
   when I consider all your commands.
[7]I will praise you with an upright heart
   as I learn your righteous laws.
[8]I will obey your decrees;
   do not utterly forsake me.

ב Beth

[9]How can a young man keep his way pure?
   By living according to your word.

---

a 26 The Hebrew is plural.
b 27 Or *Bind the festal sacrifice with ropes / and take it*
c This psalm is an acrostic poem; the verses of each stanza begin
with the same letter of the Hebrew alphabet.

¹⁰I seek you with all my heart;
　do not let me stray from your commands.
¹¹I have hidden your word in my heart
　that I might not sin against you.
¹²Praise be to you, O LORD;
　teach me your decrees.
¹³With my lips I recount
　all the laws that come from your mouth.
¹⁴I rejoice in following your statutes
　as one rejoices in great riches.
¹⁵I meditate on your precepts
　and consider your ways.
¹⁶I delight in your decrees;
　I will not neglect your word.

ℷ   Gimel

¹⁷Do good to your servant, and I will live;
　I will obey your word.
¹⁸Open my eyes that I may see
　wonderful things in your law.
¹⁹I am a stranger on earth;
　do not hide your commands from me.
²⁰My soul is consumed with longing
　for your laws at all times.
²¹You rebuke the arrogant, who are cursed
　and who stray from your commands.
²²Remove from me scorn and contempt,
　for I keep your statutes.
²³Though princes sit together and slander me,
　your servant will meditate on your decrees.
²⁴Your statutes are my delight;
　they are my counselors.

ℸ   Daleth

²⁵I am laid low in the dust;
　renew my life according to your word.
²⁶I recounted my ways and you answered me;
　teach me your decrees.
²⁷Let me understand the teaching of your precepts;
　then I will meditate on your wonders.
²⁸My soul is weary with sorrow;

strengthen me according to your word.
29Keep me from deceitful ways;
   be gracious to me through your law.
30I have chosen the way of truth;
   I have set my heart on your laws.
31I hold fast to your statutes, O LORD;
   do not let me be put to shame.
32I run in the path of your commands,
   for you have set my heart free.

ה He

33Teach me, O LORD, to follow your decrees;
   then I will keep them to the end.
34Give me understanding, and I will keep your law
   and obey it with all my heart.
35Direct me in the path of your commands,
   for there I find delight.
36Turn my heart toward your statutes
   and not toward selfish gain.
37Turn my eyes away from worthless things;
   renew my life according to your word.a
38Fulfill your promise to your servant,
   so that you may be feared.
39Take away the disgrace I dread,
   for your laws are good.
40How I long for your precepts!
   Renew my life in your righteousness.

ו Waw

41May your unfailing love come to me, O LORD,
   your salvation according to your promise;
42then I will answer the one who taunts me,
   for I trust in your word.
43Do not snatch the word of truth from my mouth,
   for I have put my hope in your laws.
44I will always obey your law,
   for ever and ever.
45I will walk about in freedom,
   for I have sought out your precepts.

a 37 Two manuscripts of the Masoretic Text and Dead Sea Scrolls;
most manuscripts of the Masoretic Text *life in your way*

⁴⁶I will speak of your statutes before kings
   and will not be put to shame,
⁴⁷for I delight in your commandments
   because I love them.
⁴⁸I reach out my hands for your commandments,
    which I love,
   and I meditate on your decrees.

ז Zayin

⁴⁹Remember your word to your servant,
   for you have given me hope.
⁵⁰My comfort in my suffering is this:
   Your promise renews my life.
⁵¹The arrogant mock me without restraint,
   but I do not turn from your law.
⁵²I remember your ancient laws, O LORD,
   and I find comfort in them.
⁵³Indignation grips me because of the wicked,
   who have forsaken your law.
⁵⁴Your decrees are the theme of my song
   wherever I lodge.
⁵⁵In the night I remember your name, O LORD,
   and I will keep your law.
⁵⁶This has been my practice:
   I obey your precepts.

ח Heth

⁵⁷You are my portion, O LORD;
   I have promised to obey your words.
⁵⁸I have sought your face with all my heart;
   be gracious to me according to your promise.
⁵⁹I have considered my ways
   and have turned my steps to your statutes.
⁶⁰I will hasten and not delay
   to obey your commands.
⁶¹Though the wicked bind me with ropes,
   I will not forget your law.
⁶²At midnight I rise to give you thanks
   for your righteous laws.
⁶³I am a friend to all who fear you,
   to all who follow your precepts.

⁶⁴The earth is filled with your love, O Lord;
　　teach me your decrees.

　　　　　　ט　Teth

⁶⁵Do good to your servant
　　according to your word, O Lord.
⁶⁶Teach me knowledge and good judgment,
　　for I believe in your commands.
⁶⁷Before I was afflicted I went astray,
　　but now I obey your word.
⁶⁸You are good, and what you do is good;
　　teach me your decrees.
⁶⁹Though the arrogant have smeared me with lies,
　　I keep your precepts with all my heart.
⁷⁰Their hearts are callous and unfeeling,
　　but I delight in your law.
⁷¹It was good for me to be afflicted
　　so that I might learn your decrees.
⁷²The law from your mouth is more precious to me
　　than thousands of pieces of silver and gold.

　　　　　　י　Yodh

⁷³Your hands made me and formed me;
　　give me understanding to learn your
　　　　commands.
⁷⁴May they who fear you rejoice when they see me,
　　for I have put my hope in your word.
⁷⁵I know, O Lord, that your laws are righteous,
　　and in faithfulness you have afflicted me.
⁷⁶May your unfailing love be my comfort,
　　according to your promise to your servant.
⁷⁷Let your compassion come to me that I may live,
　　for your law is my delight.
⁷⁸May the arrogant be put to shame for wronging
　　　　me without cause;
　　but I will meditate on your precepts.
⁷⁹May those who fear you turn to me,
　　those who understand your statutes.
⁸⁰May my heart be blameless toward your decrees,
　　that I may not be put to shame.

כ Kaph

[81]My soul faints with longing for your salvation,
    but I have put my hope in your word.
[82]My eyes fail, looking for your promise;
    I say, "When will you comfort me?"
[83]Though I am like a wineskin in the smoke,
    I do not forget your decrees.
[84]How long must your servant wait?
    When will you punish my persecutors?
[85]The arrogant dig pitfalls for me,
    contrary to your law.
[86]All your commands are trustworthy;
    help me, for men persecute me without cause.
[87]They almost wiped me from the earth,
    but I have not forsaken your precepts.
[88]Preserve my life according to your love,
    and I will obey the statutes of your mouth.

ל Lamedh

[89]Your word, O LORD, is eternal;
    it stands firm in the heavens.
[90]Your faithfulness continues through all
        generations;
    you established the earth, and it endures.
[91]Your laws endure to this day,
    for all things serve you.
[92]If your law had not been my delight,
    I would have perished in my affliction.
[93]I will never forget your precepts,
    for by them you have renewed my life.
[94]Save me, for I am yours;
    I have sought out your precepts.
[95]The wicked are waiting to destroy me,
    but I will ponder your statutes.
[96]To all perfection I see a limit;
    but your commands are boundless.

מ Mem

[97]Oh, how I love your law!
    I meditate on it all day long.
[98]Your commands make me wiser than my enemies,

for they are ever with me.

⁹⁹I have more insight than all my teachers,
    for I meditate on your statutes.

¹⁰⁰I have more understanding than the elders,
    for I obey your precepts.

¹⁰¹I have kept my feet from every evil path
    so that I might obey your word.

¹⁰²I have not departed from your laws,
    for you yourself have taught me.

¹⁰³How sweet are your promises to my taste,
    sweeter than honey to my mouth!

¹⁰⁴I gain understanding from your precepts;
    therefore I hate every wrong path.

ב Nun

¹⁰⁵Your word is a lamp to my feet
    and a light for my path.

¹⁰⁶I have taken an oath and confirmed it,
    that I will follow your righteous laws.

¹⁰⁷I have suffered much;
    renew my life, O LORD, according to your word.

¹⁰⁸Accept, O LORD, the willing praise of my mouth,
    and teach me your laws.

¹⁰⁹Though I constantly take my life in my hands,
    I will not forget your law.

¹¹⁰The wicked have set a snare for me,
    but I have not strayed from your precepts.

¹¹¹Your statutes are my heritage forever;
    they are the joy of my heart.

¹¹²My heart is set on keeping your decrees
    to the very end.

ס Samekh

¹¹³I hate double-minded men,
    but I love your law.

¹¹⁴You are my refuge and my shield;
    I have put my hope in your word.

¹¹⁵Away from me, you evildoers,
    that I may keep the commands of my God!

¹¹⁶Sustain me according to your promise, and I will
      live;

do not let my hopes be dashed.
[117]Uphold me, and I will be delivered;
    I will always have regard for your decrees.
[118]You reject all who stray from your decrees,
    for their deceitfulness is in vain.
[119]All the wicked of the earth you discard like dross;
    therefore I love your statutes.
[120]My flesh trembles in fear of you;
    I stand in awe of your laws.

ע Ayin

[121]I have done what is righteous and just;
    do not leave me to my oppressors.
[122]Ensure your servant's well-being;
    let not the arrogant oppress me.
[123]My eyes fail, looking for your salvation,
    looking for your righteous promise.
[124]Deal with your servant according to your love
    and teach me your decrees.
[125]I am your servant; give me discernment
    that I may understand your statutes.
[126]It is time for you to act, O LORD;
    your law is being broken.
[127]Because I love your commands
    more than gold, more than pure gold,
[128]and because I consider all your precepts right,
    I hate every wrong path.

פ Pe

[129]Your statutes are wonderful;
    therefore I obey them.
[130]The entrance of your words gives light;
    it gives understanding to the simple.
[131]I open my mouth and pant,
    longing for your commands.
[132]Turn to me and have mercy on me,
    as you always do to those who love your name.
[133]Direct my footsteps according to your word;
    let no sin rule over me.
[134]Redeem me from the oppression of men,
    that I may obey your precepts.

¹³⁵Make your face shine upon your servant
    and teach me your decrees.
¹³⁶Streams of tears flow from my eyes,
    for your law is not obeyed.

צ   Tsadhe

¹³⁷Righteous are you, O LORD,
    and your laws are right.
¹³⁸The statutes you have laid down are righteous;
    they are fully trustworthy.
¹³⁹My zeal wears me out,
    for my enemies ignore your words.
¹⁴⁰Your promises have been thoroughly tested,
    and your servant loves them.
¹⁴¹Though I am lowly and despised,
    I do not forget your precepts.
¹⁴²Your righteousness is everlasting
    and your law is true.
¹⁴³Trouble and distress have come upon me,
    but your commands are my delight.
¹⁴⁴Your statutes are forever right;
    give me understanding that I may live.

ק   Qoph

¹⁴⁵I call with all my heart; answer me, O LORD,
    and I will obey your decrees.
¹⁴⁶I call out to you; save me
    and I will keep your statutes.
¹⁴⁷I rise before dawn and cry for help;
    I have put my hope in your word.
¹⁴⁸My eyes stay open through the watches of the
      night,
    that I may meditate on your promises.
¹⁴⁹Hear my voice in accordance with your love;
    renew my life, O LORD, according to your laws.
¹⁵⁰Those who devise wicked schemes are near,
    but they are far from your law.
¹⁵¹Yet you are near, O LORD,
    and all your commands are true.
¹⁵²Long ago I learned from your statutes
    that you established them to last forever.

ר Resh

¹⁵³Look upon my suffering and deliver me,
for I have not forgotten your law.
¹⁵⁴Defend my cause and redeem me;
renew my life according to your promise.
¹⁵⁵Salvation is far from the wicked,
for they do not seek out your decrees.
¹⁵⁶Your compassion is great, O LORD;
renew my life according to your laws.
¹⁵⁷Many are the foes who persecute me,
but I have not turned from your statutes.
¹⁵⁸I look on the faithless with loathing,
for they do not obey your word.
¹⁵⁹See how I love your precepts;
preserve my life, O LORD, according to your
love.
¹⁶⁰All your words are true;
all your righteous laws are eternal.

שׂ Sin and Shin

¹⁶¹Rulers persecute me without cause,
but my heart trembles at your word.
¹⁶²I rejoice in your promise
like one who finds great spoil.
¹⁶³I hate and abhor falsehood
but I love your law.
¹⁶⁴Seven times a day I praise you
for your righteous laws.
¹⁶⁵Great peace have they who love your law,
and nothing can make them stumble.
¹⁶⁶I wait for your salvation, O LORD,
and I follow your commands.
¹⁶⁷I obey your statutes,
for I love them greatly.
¹⁶⁸I obey your precepts and your statutes,
for all my ways are known to you.

ת Taw

¹⁶⁹May my cry come before you, O LORD;
give me understanding according to your word.
¹⁷⁰May my supplication come before you;

deliver me according to your promise.
171May my lips overflow with praise,
for you teach me your decrees.
172May my tongue sing of your word,
for all your commands are righteous.
173May your hand be ready to help me,
for I have chosen your precepts.
174I long for your salvation, O LORD,
and your law is my delight.
175Let me live that I may praise you,
and may your laws sustain me.
176I have strayed like a lost sheep.
Seek your servant,
for I have not forgotten your commandments.

Psalm 120

A song of ascents.

1I call on the LORD in my distress,
and he answers me.
2Save me, O LORD, from lying lips
and from deceitful tongues.

3What will he do to you,
and what more besides, O deceitful tongue?
4He will punish you with a warrior's sharp arrows,
with burning coals of the broom tree.

5Woe to me that I dwell in Meshech,
that I live among the tents of Kedar!
6Too long have I lived
among those who hate peace.
7I am a man of peace;
but when I speak, they are for war.

Psalm 121

A song of ascents.

1I lift up my eyes to the hills—
where does my help come from?
2My help comes from the LORD,
the Maker of heaven and earth.

³He will not let your foot slip—
  he who watches over you will not slumber;
⁴indeed, he who watches over Israel
  will neither slumber nor sleep.

⁵The Lord watches over you—
  the Lord is your shade at your right hand;
⁶the sun will not harm you by day,
  nor the moon by night.

⁷The Lord will keep you from all harm—
  he will watch over your life;
⁸the Lord will watch over your coming and going
  both now and forevermore.

Psalm 122

A song of ascents. Of David.

¹I rejoiced with those who said to me,
  "Let us go to the house of the Lord."
²Our feet are standing
  in your gates, O Jerusalem.

³Jerusalem is built like a city
  that is closely compacted together.
⁴That is where the tribes go up,
  the tribes of the Lord,
 to praise the name of the Lord
  according to the statute given to Israel.
⁵There the thrones for judgment stand,
  the thrones of the house of David.

⁶Pray for the peace of Jerusalem:
  "May those who love you be secure.
⁷May there be peace within your walls
  and security within your citadels."
⁸For the sake of my brothers and friends,
  I will say, "Peace be within you."
⁹For the sake of the house of the Lord our God,
  I will seek your prosperity.

Psalm 123

A song of ascents.

¹I lift up my eyes to you,
    to you whose throne is in heaven.
²As the eyes of slaves look to the hand of their
        master,
    as the eyes of a maid look to the hand of her
        mistress,
 so our eyes look to the LORD our God,
    till he shows us his mercy.

³Have mercy on us, O LORD, have mercy on us,
    for we have endured much contempt.
⁴We have endured much ridicule from the proud,
    much contempt from the arrogant.

Psalm 124

A song of ascents. Of David.

¹If the LORD had not been on our side—
    let Israel say—
²if the LORD had not been on our side
    when men attacked us,
³when their anger flared against us,
    they would have swallowed us alive;
⁴the flood would have engulfed us,
    the torrent would have swept over us,
⁵   the raging waters would have swept us away.

⁶Praise be to the LORD,
    who has not let us be torn by their teeth.
⁷We have escaped like a bird
    out of the fowler's snare;
 the snare has been broken,
    and we have escaped.
⁸Our help is in the name of the LORD,
    the Maker of heaven and earth.

Psalm 125

A song of ascents.

¹Those who trust in the LORD are like Mount Zion,
   which cannot be shaken but endures forever.
²As the mountains surround Jerusalem,
   so the LORD surrounds his people
   both now and forevermore.

³The scepter of the wicked will not remain
   over the land allotted to the righteous,
for then the righteous might use
   their hands to do evil.

⁴Do good, O LORD, to those who are good,
   to those who are upright in heart.
⁵But those who turn to crooked ways
   the LORD will banish with the evildoers.

Peace be upon Israel.

Psalm 126

A song of ascents.

¹When the LORD brought back the captives to[a]
         Zion,
   we were like men who dreamed.[b]
²Our mouths were filled with laughter,
   our tongues with songs of joy.
Then it was said among the nations,
   "The LORD has done great things for them."
³The LORD has done great things for us,
   and we are filled with joy.

⁴Restore our fortunes,[c] O LORD,
   like streams in the Negev.
⁵Those who sow in tears
   will reap with songs of joy.
⁶He who goes out weeping,
   carrying seed to sow,
will return with songs of joy,
   carrying sheaves with him.

[a] 1 Or LORD *restored the fortunes of*   [b] 1 Or *men restored to health*
[c] 4 Or *Bring back our captives*

Psalm 127

A song of ascents. Of Solomon.

[1]Unless the LORD builds the house,
  its builders labor in vain.
Unless the LORD watches over the city,
  the watchmen stand guard in vain.
[2]In vain you rise early
  and stay up late,
toiling for food to eat—
  for he grants sleep to[a] those he loves.

[3]Sons are a heritage from the LORD,
  children a reward from him.
[4]Like arrows in the hands of a warrior
  are sons born in one's youth.
[5]Blessed is the man
  whose quiver is full of them.
They will not be put to shame
  when they contend with their enemies in the
      gate.

Psalm 128

A song of ascents.

[1]Blessed are all who fear the LORD,
  who walk in his ways.
[2]You will eat the fruit of your labor;
  blessings and prosperity will be yours.
[3]Your wife will be like a fruitful vine
  within your house;
your sons will be like olive shoots
  around your table.
[4]Thus is the man blessed
  who fears the LORD.

[5]May the LORD bless you from Zion
  all the days of your life;
may you see the prosperity of Jerusalem,

[a] 2 Or *eat— / for while they sleep he provides for*

6 and may you live to see your children's
    children.

Peace be upon Israel.

Psalm 129

A song of ascents.

¹They have greatly oppressed me from my youth—
    let Israel say—
²they have greatly oppressed me from my youth,
    but they have not gained the victory over me.
³Plowmen have plowed my back
    and made their furrows long.
⁴But the LORD is righteous;
    he has cut me free from the cords of the
      wicked.

⁵May all who hate Zion
    be turned back in shame.
⁶May they be like grass on the housetops,
    which withers before it can grow;
⁷with it the reaper cannot fill his hands,
    nor the one who gathers fill his arms.
⁸May those who pass by not say,
    "The blessing of the LORD be upon you;
    we bless you in the name of the LORD."

Psalm 130

A song of ascents.

¹Out of the depths I cry to you, O LORD;
²   O Lord, hear my voice.
Let your ears be attentive
    to my cry for mercy.

³If you, O LORD, kept a record of sins,
    O Lord, who could stand?
⁴But with you there is forgiveness;
    therefore you are feared.

⁵I wait for the LORD, my soul waits,
    and in his word I put my hope.

⁶My soul waits for the Lord
   more than watchmen wait for the morning,
   more than watchmen wait for the morning.

⁷O Israel, put your hope in the LORD,
   for with the LORD is unfailing love
   and with him is full redemption.
⁸He himself will redeem Israel
   from all their sins.

Psalm 131

A song of ascents. Of David.

¹My heart is not proud, O LORD,
   my eyes are not haughty;
 I do not concern myself with great matters
   or things too wonderful for me.
²But I have stilled and quieted my soul;
   like a weaned child with its mother,
   like a weaned child is my soul within me.

³O Israel, put your hope in the LORD
   both now and forevermore.

Psalm 132

A song of ascents.

¹O LORD, remember David
   and all the hardships he endured.

²He swore an oath to the LORD
   and made a vow to the Mighty One of Jacob:
³"I will not enter my house
   or go to my bed—
⁴I will allow no sleep to my eyes,
   no slumber to my eyelids,
⁵till I find a place for the LORD,
   a dwelling for the Mighty One of Jacob."

⁶We heard it in Ephrathah,

we came upon it in the fields of Jaar[a]:[b]
[7]"Let us go to his dwelling place;
let us worship at his footstool—
[8]arise, O LORD, and come to your resting place,
you and the ark of your might.
[9]May your priests be clothed with righteousness;
may your saints sing for joy."

[10]For the sake of David your servant,
do not reject your anointed one.

[11]The LORD swore an oath to David,
a sure oath that he will not revoke:
"One of your own descendants
I will place on your throne—
[12]if your sons keep my covenant
and the statutes I teach them,
then their sons will sit
on your throne for ever and ever."

[13]For the LORD has chosen Zion,
he has desired it for his dwelling:
[14]"This is my resting place for ever and ever;
here I will sit enthroned, for I have desired it—
[15]I will bless her with abundant provisions;
her poor will I satisfy with food.
[16]I will clothe her priests with salvation,
and her saints will ever sing for joy.

[17]"Here I will make a horn[c] grow for David
and set up a lamp for my anointed one.
[18]I will clothe his enemies with shame,
but the crown on his head will be resplendent."

Psalm 133

A song of ascents. Of David.

[1]How good and pleasant it is
when brothers live together in unity!
[2]It is like precious oil poured on the head,

[a] 6 That is, Kiriath Jearim
[b] 6 Or *heard of it in Ephrathah, / we found it in the fields of Jaar.* (And
no quotes around verses 7-9)
[c] 17 *Horn* here symbolizes strong one, that is, king.

running down on the beard,
running down on Aaron's beard,
    down upon the collar of his robes.
³It is as if the dew of Hermon
    were falling on Mount Zion.
For there the LORD bestows his blessing,
    even life forevermore.

Psalm 134

A song of ascents.

¹Praise the LORD, all you servants of the LORD
    who minister by night in the house of the
        LORD.
²Lift up your hands in the sanctuary
    and praise the LORD.

³May the LORD, the Maker of heaven and earth,
    bless you from Zion.

Psalm 135

¹Praise the LORD.ᵃ

Praise the name of the LORD;
    Praise him, you servants of the LORD,
²you who minister in the house of the LORD,
    in the courts of the house of our God.

³Praise the LORD, for the LORD is good;
    sing praise to his name, for that is pleasant.
⁴For the LORD has chosen Jacob to be his own,
    Israel to be his treasured possession.

⁵I know that the LORD is great,
    that our Lord is greater than all gods.
⁶The LORD does whatever pleases him,
    in the heavens and on the earth,
    in the seas and all their depths.
⁷He makes clouds rise from the ends of the earth;
    he sends lightning with the rain
    and brings out the wind from his storehouses.

ᵃ1 Hebrew *Hallelu Yah*; also in verses 3 and 21

⁸He struck down the firstborn of Egypt,
   the firstborn of men and animals.
⁹He sent his signs and wonders into your midst, O
       Egypt,
   against Pharaoh and all his servants.
¹⁰He struck down many nations
   and killed mighty kings—
¹¹Sihon king of the Amorites,
   Og king of Bashan
   and all the kings of Canaan—
¹²and he gave their land as an inheritance,
   an inheritance to his people Israel.

¹³Your name, O LORD, endures forever,
   your renown, O LORD, through all generations.
¹⁴For the LORD will vindicate his people
   and have compassion on his servants.

¹⁵The idols of the nations are silver and gold,
   made by the hands of men.
¹⁶They have mouths, but cannot speak,
   eyes, but they cannot see;
¹⁷they have ears, but cannot hear,
   nor is there breath in their mouths.
¹⁸Those who make them will be like them,
   and so will all who trust in them.

¹⁹O house of Israel, praise the LORD;
   O house of Aaron, praise the LORD;
²⁰O house of Levi, praise the LORD;
   you who fear him, praise the LORD.
²¹Praise be to the LORD from Zion,
   to him who dwells in Jerusalem.

Praise the LORD.

Psalm 136

¹Give thanks to the LORD, for he is good.
                    His love endures forever.
²Give thanks to the God of gods.
                    His love endures forever.
³Give thanks to the Lord of lords:
                    His love endures forever.

⁴to him who alone does great wonders,
His love endures forever.
⁵who by his understanding made the heavens,
His love endures forever.
⁶who spread out the earth upon the waters,
His love endures forever.
⁷who made the great lights—
His love endures forever.
⁸the sun to govern the day,
His love endures forever.
⁹the moon and stars to govern the night;
His love endures forever.

¹⁰to him who struck down the firstborn of Egypt
His love endures forever.
¹¹and brought Israel out from among them
His love endures forever.
¹²with a mighty hand and outstretched arm;
His love endures forever.

¹³to him who divided the Red Sea[a] asunder
His love endures forever.
¹⁴and brought Israel through the midst of it,
His love endures forever.
¹⁵but swept Pharaoh and his army into the Red Sea;
His love endures forever.

¹⁶to him who led his people through the desert,
His love endures forever.
¹⁷who struck down great kings,
His love endures forever.
¹⁸and killed mighty kings—
His love endures forever.
¹⁹Sihon king of the Amorites
His love endures forever.
²⁰and Og king of Bashan—
His love endures forever.
²¹and gave their land as an inheritance,
His love endures forever.
²²an inheritance to his servant Israel;
His love endures forever.

[a] 13 Hebrew *Yam Suph;* that is, Sea of Reeds; also in verse 15

²³to the One who remembered us in our low estate
His love endures forever.
²⁴and freed us from our enemies,
His love endures forever.
²⁵and who gives food to every creature.
His love endures forever.

²⁶Give thanks to the God of heaven.
His love endures forever.

Psalm 137

¹By the rivers of Babylon we sat and wept
when we remembered Zion.
²There on the poplars
we hung our harps,
³for there our captors asked us for songs,
our tormentors demanded songs of joy;
they said, "Sing us one of the songs of Zion!"

⁴How can we sing the songs of the LORD
while in a foreign land?
⁵If I forget you, O Jerusalem,
may my right hand forget its skill.
⁶May my tongue cling to the roof of my mouth
if I do not remember you,
if I do not consider Jerusalem
my highest joy.

⁷Remember, O LORD, what the Edomites did
on the day Jerusalem fell.
"Tear it down," they cried,
"tear it down to its foundations!"

⁸O Daughter of Babylon, doomed to destruction,
happy is he who repays you
for what you have done to us—
⁹he who seizes your infants
and dashes them against the rocks.

Psalm 138

Of David.

¹I will praise you, O LORD, with all my heart;
  before the "gods" I will sing your praise.
²I will bow down toward your holy temple
  and will praise your name
  for your love and your faithfulness,
for you have exalted above all things
  your name and your word.
³When I called, you answered me;
  you made me bold and stouthearted.

⁴May all the kings of the earth praise you, O LORD,
  when they hear the words of your mouth.
⁵May they sing of the ways of the LORD,
  for the glory of the LORD is great.

⁶Though the LORD is on high, he looks upon the
      lowly,
  but the proud he knows from afar.
⁷Though I walk in the midst of trouble,
  you preserve my life;
you stretch out your hand against the anger of my
      foes,
  with your right hand you save me.
⁸The LORD will fulfill ⌊his purpose⌋ for me;
  your love, O LORD, endures forever—
  do not abandon the works of your hands.

Psalm 139

For the director of music. Of David. A psalm.

¹O LORD, you have searched me
  and you know me.
²You know when I sit and when I rise;
  you perceive my thoughts from afar.
³You discern my going out and my lying down;
  you are familiar with all my ways.
⁴Before a word is on my tongue
  you know it completely, O LORD.

⁵You hem me in, behind and before;

you have laid your hand upon me.
⁶Such knowledge is too wonderful for me,
  too lofty for me to attain.

⁷Where can I go from your Spirit?
  Where can I flee from your presence?
⁸If I go up to the heavens, you are there;
  if I make my bed in the depths,ᵃ you are there.
⁹If I rise on the wings of the dawn,
  if I settle on the far side of the sea,
¹⁰even there your hand will guide me,
  your right hand will hold me fast.

¹¹If I say, "Surely the darkness will hide me
  and the light become night around me,"
¹²even the darkness will not be dark to you;
  the night will shine like the day,
  for darkness is as light to you.

¹³For you created my inmost being;
  you knit me together in my mother's womb.
¹⁴I praise you because I am fearfully and
      wonderfully made;
  your works are wonderful,
  I know that full well.
¹⁵My frame was not hidden from you
  when I was made in the secret place.
When I was woven together in the depths of the
     earth,
¹⁶ your eyes saw my unformed body.
All the days ordained for me
  were written in your book
  before one of them came to be.

¹⁷How precious toᵇ me are your thoughts, O God!
  How vast is the sum of them!
¹⁸Were I to count them,
  they would outnumber the grains of sand.
When I awake,
  I am still with you.

¹⁹If only you would slay the wicked, O God!

ᵃ 8 Hebrew *Sheol*   ᵇ 17 Or *concerning*

Away from me, you bloodthirsty men!
²⁰They speak of you with evil intent;
    your adversaries misuse your name.
²¹Do I not hate those who hate you, O LORD,
    and abhor those who rise up against you?
²²I have nothing but hatred for them;
    I count them my enemies.

²³Search me, O God, and know my heart;
    test me and know my anxious thoughts.
²⁴See if there is any offensive way in me,
    and lead me in the way everlasting.

Psalm 140

For the director of music. A psalm of David.

¹Rescue me, O LORD, from evil men;
    protect me from men of violence,
²who devise evil plans in their hearts
    and stir up war every day.
³They make their tongues as sharp as a serpent's;
    the poison of vipers is on their lips.   *Selah*

⁴Keep me, O LORD, from the hands of the wicked;
    protect me from men of violence
    who plan to trip my feet.
⁵Proud men have hidden a snare for me;
    they have spread out the cords of their net
    and have set traps for me along my path.   *Selah*

⁶O LORD, I say to you, "You are my God."
    Hear, O LORD, my cry for mercy.
⁷O Sovereign LORD, my strong deliverer,
    who shields my head in the day of battle—
⁸do not grant the wicked their desires, O LORD;
    do not let their plans succeed,
    or they will become proud.   *Selah*

⁹Let the heads of those who surround me
    be covered with the trouble their lips have
        caused.
¹⁰Let burning coals fall upon them;
    may they be thrown into the fire,

.into miry pits, never to rise.
[11]Let slanderers not be established in the land;
    may disaster hunt down men of violence.

[12]I know that the LORD secures justice for the poor
    and upholds the cause of the needy.
[13]Surely the righteous will praise your name
    and the upright will live before you.

Psalm 141

A psalm of David.

[1]O LORD, I call to you; come quickly to me.
    Hear my voice when I call to you.
[2]May my prayer be set before you like incense;
    may the lifting up of my hands be like the
        evening sacrifice.

[3]Set a guard over my mouth, O LORD;
    keep watch over the door of my lips.
[4]Let not my heart be drawn to what is evil,
    to take part in wicked deeds
with men who are evildoers;
    let me not eat of their delicacies.

[5]Let a righteous man strike me—it is a kindness;
    let him rebuke me—it is oil on my head.
    My head will not refuse it.

Yet my prayer is ever against the deeds of
    evildoers;
[6] their rulers will be thrown down from the
    cliffs,
    and the wicked will learn that my words were
        well spoken.
[7]They will say, "As one plows and breaks up the
    earth,
    so our bones have been scattered at the mouth
        of the grave.[a]"

[8]But my eyes are fixed on you, O Sovereign LORD;

---

[a]7 Hebrew *Sheol*

in you I take refuge—do not give me over to
   death.
⁹Keep me from the snares they have laid for me,
   from the traps set by evildoers.
¹⁰Let the wicked fall into their own nets,
   while I pass by in safety.

Psalm 142

A *maskil*[a] of David. When he was in the cave. A prayer.

¹I cry aloud to the LORD;
   I lift up my voice to the LORD for mercy.
²I pour out my complaint before him;
   before him I tell my trouble.

³When my spirit grows faint within me,
   it is you who know my way.
In the path where I walk
   men have hidden a snare for me.
⁴Look to my right and see;
   no one is concerned for me.
I have no refuge;
   no one cares for my life.

⁵I cry to you, O LORD;
   I say, "You are my refuge,
   my portion in the land of the living."
⁶Listen to my cry,
   for I am in desperate need;
rescue me from those who pursue me,
   for they are too strong for me.
⁷Set me free from my prison
   that I may praise your name.

Then the righteous will gather about me
   because of your goodness to me.

[a] Title: Probably a literary or musical term

Psalm 143

A psalm of David.

¹O Lᴏʀᴅ, hear my prayer,
    listen to my cry for mercy;
in your faithfulness and righteousness
    come to my relief.
²Do not bring your servant into judgment,
    for no one living is righteous before you.

³The enemy pursues me,
    he crushes me to the ground;
he makes me dwell in darkness
    like those long dead.
⁴So my spirit grows faint within me;
    my heart within me is dismayed.

⁵I remember the days of long ago;
    I meditate on all your works
    and consider what your hands have done.
⁶I spread out my hands to you;
    my soul thirsts for you like a parched land. *Selah*

⁷Answer me quickly, O Lᴏʀᴅ;
    my spirit faints with longing.
Do not hide your face from me
    or I will be like those who go down to the pit.
⁸Let the morning bring me word of your unfailing
        love,
    for I have put my trust in you.
Show me the way I should go,
    for to you I lift up my soul.
⁹Rescue me from my enemies, O Lᴏʀᴅ,
    for I hide myself in you.
¹⁰Teach me to do your will,
    for you are my God;
may your good Spirit
    lead me on level ground.

¹¹For your name's sake, O Lᴏʀᴅ, preserve my life;
    in your righteousness, bring me out of trouble.
¹²In your unfailing love, silence my enemies;
    destroy all my foes,
    for I am your servant.

Psalm 144

Of David.

¹Praise be to the LORD, my Rock,
   who trains my hands for war,
   my fingers for battle.
²He is my loving God and my fortress,
   my stronghold and my deliverer,
my shield, in whom I take refuge,
   who subdues peoplesª under me.

³O LORD, what is man that you care for him,
   the son of man that you think of him?
⁴Man is like a breath;
   his days are like a fleeting shadow.

⁵Part your heavens, O LORD, and come down;
   touch the mountains, so that they smoke.
⁶Send forth lightning and scatter ⌊the enemies⌋;
   shoot your arrows and rout them.
⁷Reach down your hand from on high;
   deliver me and rescue me
from the mighty waters,
   from the hands of foreigners
⁸whose mouths are full of lies,
   whose right hands are deceitful.

⁹I will sing a new song to you, O God;
   on the ten-stringed lyre I will make music to
      you,
¹⁰to the One who gives victory to kings,
   who delivers his servant David from the deadly
      sword.

¹¹Deliver me and rescue me
   from the hands of foreigners
whose mouths are full of lies,
   whose right hands are deceitful.
¹²Then our sons in their youth
   will be like well-nurtured plants,

ª 2 Many manuscripts of the Masoretic Text, Dead Sea Scrolls,
Aquila, Jerome and Syriac; most manuscripts of the Masoretic
Text *subdues my people*

and our daughters will be like pillars
    carved to adorn a palace.
13Our barns will be filled
    with every kind of provision.
Our sheep will increase by thousands,
    by tens of thousands in our fields;
14   our oxen will draw heavy loads.[a]
There will be no breaching of walls,
    no going into captivity,
    no cry of distress in our streets.

15Blessed are the people of whom this is true;
    blessed are the people whose God is the Lord.

Psalm 145[b]

A psalm of praise. Of David.

1I will exalt you, my God the King;
    I will praise your name for ever and ever.
2Every day I will praise you
    and extol your name for ever and ever.

3Great is the Lord and most worthy of praise;
    his greatness no one can fathom.
4One generation will commend your works to
        another;
    they will tell of your mighty acts.
5They will speak of the glorious splendor of your
        majesty,
    and I will meditate on your wonderful works.[c]
6They will tell of the power of your awesome
        works,
    and I will proclaim your great deeds.
7They will celebrate your abundant goodness
    and joyfully sing of your righteousness.

---

[a] 14 Or *our chieftains will be firmly established*
[b] This psalm is an acrostic poem, the verses of which (including
verse 13b) begin with the successive letters of the Hebrew
alphabet.
[c] 5 Dead Sea Scrolls and Syriac (see also Septuagint); Masoretic
Text *On the glorious splendor of your majesty / and on your wonderful
works I will meditate*

⁸The LORD is gracious and compassionate,
    slow to anger and rich in love.
⁹The LORD is good to all;
    he has compassion on all he has made.
¹⁰All you have made will praise you, O LORD;
    your saints will extol you.
¹¹They will tell of the glory of your kingdom
    and speak of your might,
¹²so that all men may know of your mighty acts
    and the glorious splendor of your kingdom.
¹³Your kingdom is an everlasting kingdom,
    and your dominion endures through all
        generations.

  The LORD is faithful to all his promises
    and loving toward all he has made.ᵃ
¹⁴The LORD upholds all those who fall
    and lifts up all who are bowed down.
¹⁵The eyes of all look to you,
    and you give them their food at the proper
        time.
¹⁶You open your hand
    and satisfy the desires of every living
        thing.

¹⁷The LORD is righteous in all his ways
    and loving toward all he has made.
¹⁸The LORD is near to all who call on him,
    to all who call on him in truth.
¹⁹He fulfills the desires of those who fear him;
    he hears their cry and saves them.
²⁰The LORD watches over all who love him,
    but all the wicked he will destroy.

²¹My mouth will speak in praise of the LORD.
    Let every creature praise his holy name
    for ever and ever.

ᵃ13 One manuscript of the Masoretic Text, Dead Sea Scrolls,
Septuagint and Syriac; most manuscripts of the Masoretic Text do
not have the last two lines of verse 13.

Psalm 146

[1]Praise the LORD.[a]

Praise the LORD, O my soul.
2   I will praise the LORD all my life;
    I will sing praise to my God as long as I live.

[3]Do not put your trust in princes,
    in mortal men, who cannot save.
[4]When their spirit departs, they return to the
        ground;
    on that very day their plans come to
        nothing.

[5]Blessed is he whose help is the God of Jacob,
    whose hope is in the LORD his God,
[6]the Maker of heaven and earth,
    the sea, and everything in them—
    the LORD, who remains faithful forever.
[7]He upholds the cause of the oppressed
    and gives food to the hungry.
The LORD sets prisoners free,
8   the LORD gives sight to the blind,
    the LORD lifts up those who are bowed down,
    the LORD loves the righteous.
[9]The LORD watches over the alien
    and sustains the fatherless and the widow,
    but he frustrates the ways of the wicked.

[10]The LORD reigns forever,
    your God, O Zion, for all generations.

    Praise the LORD.

Psalm 147

[1]Praise the LORD.[b]

How good it is to sing praises to our God,
    how pleasant and fitting to praise him!

a 1 Hebrew *Hallelu Yah*; also in verse 10
b 1 Hebrew *Hallelu Yah*; also in verse 20

²The LORD builds up Jerusalem;
    he gathers the exiles of Israel.
³He heals the brokenhearted
    and binds up their wounds.

⁴He determines the number of the stars
    and calls them each by name.
⁵Great is our Lord and mighty in power;
    his understanding has no limit.
⁶The LORD sustains the humble
    but casts the wicked to the ground.

⁷Sing to the LORD with thanksgiving;
    make music to our God on the harp.
⁸He covers the sky with clouds;
    he supplies the earth with rain
    and makes grass grow on the hills.
⁹He provides food for the cattle
    and for the young ravens when they call.

¹⁰His pleasure is not in the strength of the horse,
    nor his delight in the legs of a man;
¹¹the LORD delights in those who fear him,
    who put their hope in his unfailing love.

¹²Extol the LORD, O Jerusalem;
    praise your God, O Zion,
¹³for he strengthens the bars of your gates
    and blesses your people within you.
¹⁴He grants peace to your borders
    and satisfies you with the finest of wheat.

¹⁵He sends his command to the earth;
    his word runs swiftly.
¹⁶He spreads the snow like wool
    and scatters the frost like ashes.
¹⁷He hurls down his hail like pebbles.
    Who can withstand his icy blast?
¹⁸He sends his word and melts them;
    he stirs up his breezes, and the waters flow.

¹⁹He has revealed his word to Jacob,
    his laws and decrees to Israel.

²⁰He has done this for no other nation;
　　they do not know his laws.

Praise the LORD.

Psalm 148

¹Praise the LORD.^a

Praise the LORD from the heavens,
　　praise him in the heights above.
²Praise him, all his angels,
　　praise him, all his heavenly hosts.
³Praise him, sun and moon,
　　praise him, all you shining stars.
⁴Praise him, you highest heavens
　　and you waters above the skies.
⁵Let them praise the name of the LORD,
　　for he commanded and they were created.
⁶He set them in place for ever and ever;
　　he gave a decree that will never pass away.

⁷Praise the LORD from the earth,
　　you great sea creatures and all ocean
　　　　depths,
⁸lightning and hail, snow and clouds,
　　stormy winds that do his bidding,
⁹you mountains and all hills,
　　fruit trees and all cedars,
¹⁰wild animals and all cattle,
　　small creatures and flying birds,
¹¹kings of the earth and all nations,
　　you princes and all rulers on earth,
¹²young men and maidens,
　　old men and children.

¹³Let them praise the name of the LORD,
　　for his name alone is exalted;
　　his splendor is above the earth and the
　　　　heavens.
¹⁴He has raised up for his people a horn,^b

^a 1 Hebrew *Hallelu Yah*; also in verse 14
^b 14 *Horn* here symbolizes strong one, that is, king.

the praise of all his saints,
of Israel, the people close to his heart.

Praise the LORD.

Psalm 149

[1]Praise the LORD.[a]

Sing to the LORD a new song,
his praise in the assembly of the saints.

[2]Let Israel rejoice in their Maker;
let the people of Zion be glad in their King.
[3]Let them praise his name with dancing
and make music to him with tambourine and
harp.
[4]For the LORD takes delight in his people;
he crowns the humble with salvation.
[5]Let the saints rejoice in this honor
and sing for joy on their beds.

[6]May the praise of God be in their mouths
and a double-edged sword in their hands,
[7]to inflict vengeance on the nations
and punishment on the peoples,
[8]to bind their kings with fetters,
their nobles with shackles of iron,
[9]to carry out the sentence written against them.
This is the glory of all his saints.

Praise the LORD.

Psalm 150

[1]Praise the LORD.[b]

Praise God in his sanctuary;
praise him in his mighty heavens.
[2]Praise him for his acts of power;
praise him for his surpassing greatness.
[3]Praise him with the sounding of the trumpet,
praise him with the harp and lyre,

a 1 Hebrew *Hallelu Yah*; also in verse 9
b 1 Hebrew *Hallelu Yah*; also in verse 6

⁴praise him with tambourine and dancing,
    praise him with the strings and flute,
⁵praise him with the clash of cymbals,
    praise him with resounding cymbals.
⁶Let everything that has breath praise the LORD.

Praise the LORD.